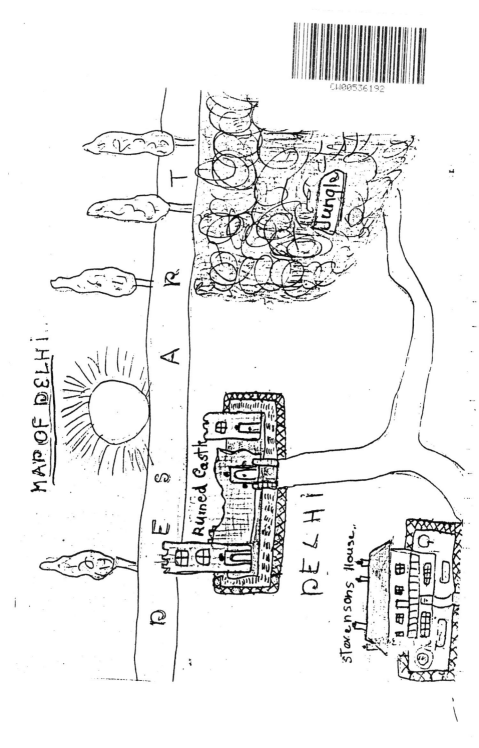

MAP OF DELHI

DESART

Jungle

Ruined Castle

DELHI

Stevenson's House.

Iona aged 2

Black Sea Bride

Iona Wright

A SQUARE ONE PUBLICATION

First published in 1997 by
Square One Publications,
The Tudor House
Upton upon Severn, Worcs. WR8 0HT

Reprinted 2001

British Cataloguing Data is available for this title

ISBN 1 899955 25 9

Typeset in Palatino 11 on 13 by Avon Dataset Ltd,
Bidford-on-Avon, Warwickshire, B50 4JH

Printed by Biddles Short Run Books, Kings Lynn, England

For Denis

"They had met, and included in their meeting, the thrust of the manifold grass-stems, the cry of the peewit, the wheel of the stars."

D. H. Lawrence
Sons and Lovers

Contents

First Years

In April 1912, when the great liner, the **Titanic**, sailed out of Belfast Lough on her maiden voyage, I was six months old, and my mother held me up to watch it from her house in Craigavad, a wealthy suburb of Belfast, overlooking the Lough. It was the pride of the Protestant community and its loss was a tremendous blow to them; two further ships that were planned were never made. My father had trained to be an electrical engineer in Harland and Wolff's ship-yard. He was the youngest of eight sons of James Craig, a Director of Dunvilles Whisky Distillery, who wanted all of his sons to have a career, but when he died in 1900, leaving them all a great deal of money, some went into politics, one into the linen business, and the rest decided to live the life of 'country gentlemen'. My father and his next eldest brother between them bought a fishing boat and turned it into a comfortable steam yacht, in which they went frequently to Scotland, and finally as far as St. Petersburg. On this last trip my mother and her twin sister, and their father and mother, were guests. The Craig brothers had deputed their only sister, married to a London solicitor, to find them two pretty girls, and she had chosen the twin daughters of her husband's partner, then living in Surrey; the result was that Molly and Patty Howell married Edwin and Granville Craig. Mrs Howell, who had six children in all, must have been delighted for two of them to have found rich husbands, but their father, a Liberal, doubted their

1

enthusiasm for the highly conservative and conventional Belfast society of families leading the three industries of whisky, linen and shipbuilding. They were only twenty years old and soon missed the company of their brothers and sister, with whom they had enjoyed a life of sport, dancing and music. On her arrival in her home in Craigavad my mother found the cupboards filled with arms, stored to fight the South. She did not like Sir Edward Carson, who in the year that I was born, became head of the Ulster Unionists, and was a close friend of the Craigs. She lost her first child, Carmen, who died when only a week old and is buried in the small churchyard at Tyrella, County Down, where old James Craig had a country house, two storeyed, large and rambling, with tall windows overlooking Dundrum Bay; with the mountains of Morne in the background, and the sea at the bottom of the garden, I can imagine how my mother must have loved Tyrella.

She had a friend in Ireland, sympathetic to the South, as she was. "Linnet" Buxton, one of the Norfolk family, had married my mother's cousin Philip Howell, a soldier in the British army at the Curragh camp. And in 1913, when I was two years old, my mother and father moved to England and to Norfolk, near to Linnet's family home at Fritton, Great Yarmouth. My mother had always been homesick and now she was nearer her own family, although the Craigs had always treated her with kindness. Edwin and Molly had also moved, to Surrey. We settled in Hopton-on-Sea, near Lowestoft and Great Yarmouth, and my father was to buy a fishing boat and join the fishing fleet, but the Great War intervened.

He had been in the Boer War, joining the Ulster Rifles as a very young man, together with an elder brother; it had been a great adventure and he had taken many photographs. In 1903, with his brother Edwin he had been round the world, describing in his diary every train and ship they travelled in, their speeds and the weather they encountered, but though they attended the great Delhi Durbar held by Curzon he did not comment on what must have been a magnificent spectacle, or mention any Indians they had met. But this was the last

2

time he found much pleasure in leaving home. In 1914 he joined the Royal Flying Corps, but was only in the balloon division, and became ill, so that he was for a time in a hospital in Italy and then was invalided home, to become a Special Constable in Norfolk, which was expecting an invasion. "Pill-boxes" were built in the fields between us and the sea and my nurse, a townswoman, was not sure of what she was most afraid, cows which we might encounter on our walks, or Germans!

My father set himself up a workshop in a coach house next to our garage; it was full of tools and a long bench, and had a particular smell of wood, steel and oil. It was sad that he had no son to share it with; my three sisters were born in 1916, 1917 and 1920. He taught us to make our rabbit hutches. He also bought the chassis of a Delage car and made the body himself, painting the wooden sides blue with a narrow yellow line round the top, but as he did not make doors we had to climb in with the help of a step.

My mother, once again in a Conservative environment, had changed her views from Liberal to Fabian Socialist. She invited James Maxton of the I.L.P., and Ishbel Macdonald, to come and stay and address meetings; my father did not object, and liked them. But he remained a Conservative and refused to let my mother use the car for her meetings, she had to go by bicycle, and once when she hired a pony and trap from a local farmer, she found that it drew her up to every pub on the way.

But one result of her socialist views was that she antagonised the people with whom my father would have been friendly, apart from a family living in Hopton House connected with Barclays Bank in Yarmouth, where her friend Linnet's brother also worked. My father was a shy man. Once as a boy travelling back from school in England on the ferry to Belfast, he saw one of his older brothers on board but did not dare to approach him. In Norfolk he did not make friends for himself, but worked alone all day at home, one of his few contacts being Mr Middleton of Yarmouth, our builder, with whom he could discuss for hours, problems of heating, drainage, etc. Mr

3

Manor Close, Hopton-on-Sea in Norfolk.

Middleton was a travelled man, every year he would go somewhere in Europe and send me a postcard – 'Budapest, nice place, H. Middleton'.

Another result of my mother's activities was that as we were four children who could very well play together, she did not take us to children's parties – given usually by Conservatives – in the neighbourhood, or give them herself, so that we became almost as shy as my father, and covered this up by asserting that we did not *like* other children, I wrote in a book called *Us*, "We hate having parties and do all we can to avoid other children; it has become a custom to get behind a hedge when we see them coming our way."

In the summer months we were joined by many relatives, to enjoy our sea-side – the 'golden sands' of Norfolk, and it was during one of these visits that I, playing excitedly with two older cousins who were trying to make a cave in the cliff, was hit by a boulder when the roof fell in. Taken to a small bedroom at the top of our house which I was occupying while we had guests, I told my mother, waiting anxiously for the doctor to arrive from Yarmouth, that I wanted to die. But after an alarming X-ray, in the dark, with nurses in masks and lights crackling and sparkling all round, it was found that I had a broken pelvis and would have to lie on my back for six months, after which I could be taken out in a push-chair by my sisters' nurse; I was eight years old, and during the time spent lying down I was taken on our annual visit to my mother's twin sister and her husband, Edwin, who lived with their two children in Surrey. We all looked forward to this trip in the Delage through Ipswich and London, to turning down their steep drive and entering the large, cool central hall smelling of beeswax and flowers, which led through a drawing-room to a gold-fish pool and sloping lawns. Nearby lived another uncle, my godfather, a great reader who always sent me a book for my birthday. Hearing of my accident he sent me *The Schoolgirls Annual* with the inscription 'To the plucky Iona', of which I was obviously too proud, as I stuck my bookplate over it, but noted that it could still be read when held up to the light.

He had also given me beautiful editions of *Gulliver's Travels* and *Tom Sawyer*. While lying down I read, or had read to me, the works of Harriet Martineau and Mrs Ewing, and sentimental tales by the S.P.C.K. such as *Us and our donkey*; my favourites were *Jackanapes, a story of a short life* by Mrs Ewing, *Little Lord Fauntleroy* and *The Princess and Curdie* and *Little Princess*. These were all emotional stories, sometimes sad and frightening, but what really intrigued and stimulated me were those by E. Nesbit, particularly *The Treasure Seekers*; the Indian uncle suggested to me our own uncle, one of my mother's brothers who was in the army in India. I wrote a story myself about the Indian mutiny called *The Stevensons in India*, in which Mr Stevenson was 'put in prison in Delhi and it was awfull.'

Once recovered I was given my own room and a large

Going to Colorado 1925. Eleanor, Priscilla, Ailsa and Iona.

bookcase with a cupboard below in which I locked up my dolls so that my sisters – who I referred to as 'the babies' because I was the elder by five years – could not get them. I filled the bookcase, arranging and re-arranging it, talking as I did so. "Now *Lang's Fairy Tales*, you go next to *Peter Pan*", and so on; I believed in fairies and treasured a small book illustrated by photographs called *Finding a Fairy*, in which one could see, in trees, mysterious shapes. I possessed a small stuffed doll with flaxen hair, only four inches tall called Henrietta to whom I talked to at night and pretended that she lived in a hole in an old church tower which we passed on the way to school.

Soon after this I came across the books of Zane Grey, and a passion for travel, particularly in America, began. After reading *Riders of the Purple Sage* I invented a game we all played, called "Going to Colorado." In "*Us*", written when I was fifteen, I say:–

"About four years ago I read an exciting book by Zane Grey about Colorado, and was so impressed by the description

6

of that state that I told Asa and Enna and Prill about it and we decided that if we could go as far as America we would go there. Then, I read a description of Utah, a neighbouring state, in the American National Geographic Magazine . . . we decided it was even better than Colorado as it was much wilder and the scenery of the Grand Canyon was the most wonderful in Utah. We saw a photo of a valley which we want to make the object of our expedition. So now Utah is our ambition and our idea is to go with a tent, a canoe, and a month's requirements. Really, just us four want to go with a servant, but I'm afraid that would not be allowed (by our parents). We should go on horses with three extra ones for equipment and we should wear cowboy clothes, we are all so keen on it that we have constant rehearsals in the garden though we do not sleep out . . . Our meals consist of biscuits and baked potatoes . . . We undress as far as stays and combinations and then put on our nightdresses or pyjamas. The bother is that we always get so frightfully hot in the tent. Once we made our camp in a field and saw a party of tourists in the old church which adjoins it. Our strange appearance in nightdresses at 3 p.m. evidently attracted them . . . We at once assumed they were Mormons (who abound in Utah) . . . and made quite an exciting story out of it."

Games such as "Colorado" filled the time in which we should have been playing with other children . . .

"We walked down the lane and then suddenly decided to explore an old pond hidden in trees and bushes. We got scratched and stung but had an exciting time. Emerging on the road again we surveyed our clothing which was rather scanty. We had no socks or stockings, and old sandals on, our tunics were dusty and green in some places where we had rubbed against trees. We had old blouses which were much too small, which had very short sleeves and would not do up at the neck, and we were hatless. It was a Sunday and many people were going to the beach. We decided to go home quickly and avoid meeting someone we knew. But before we could reach our gate along came a party of people whom we recognised to be the daughter, son-in-law and grandchildren* of a very respectable and old fashioned family who lived at Hopton House. It was impossible to escape so I had to walk up and speak to them. They all looked horrified at our clothing and at first did not seem to recognise us. When they did the son-in-law said 'Goodness what awful scratches you have got on your legs' and his wife said 'You poor things you ought to have them bandaged up'. We protested but it was no use. They insisted on our going home at once and bathing them. We did the going home part, but not the other. Their children had on silk socks, walking shoes, white dresses and white bonnets."

We all went to a school called St. Christopher's in Lowestoft, where I started at the age of seven and there were only seven pupils. But my mother supplied desks and a P.N.E.U.** curriculum, on which she was very keen, and the school flourished and grew. It was run by Miss Rose, an elderly (to us) spinster with a curled fringe of hair like Queen Mary and high, boned collars. As my mother was her benefactor she favoured us in every way and at the age of ten I was in the fifth form among girls much older than myself, although not so much more intelligent as to be stimulating because although my mother could provide books she could not ensure that the teachers would use them well. On Sundays and in the early mornings before we left for school, she would join us in the nursery to conduct prayers and play hymns and we also attended the village Sunday school where she officiated, and belonged to the Girl Guides and Brownies.

We had lunch at school and in the spare half hour before it

*One of whom was Francis Pym, later Foreign Secretary under Mrs Thatcher.
** Parents National Educational Union.

we were free to go off into town and buy sweets and weekly papers. Sometimes we went to an improvised cricket pitch where the girls' brothers from the boys Secondary school would be practising. They did not allow us to play but they came over and chatted to us so that we began to think we would end by marrying them. A dark, mischievous boy called Fred used to write me letters whenever he could not be there, and he even bicycled along the cliffs to our house and waited for me to signal with a bath-towel if I could not manage to meet him, but I was usually more amused by a less demonstrative friend of his called 'Tishy', who was supposed to be fond of someone else.

The papers I bought were *The School Friend* and the *Schoolgirls Own*, sister to the *Boys Own* and I used to pretend I was in a dormitory at night and talk to other girls, until my mother decided to send me to the P.N.E.U. boarding school in Burgess Hill, Sussex, at the age of fourteen, and I have always been grateful to her for not taking me away again when I decided I did not like it. I had been spoilt in many ways after the death of baby Carmen, and she might have given in to me, but as it was she persuaded me to stay and make friends; and one advantage of boarding school is also the excitement of coming home again, something which the 'foreign' children from overseas could sadly not experience before the days of aeroplanes. For many holidays my mother cared for a niece from India, whom we resented and despised because she could not climb trees, and I had a guilty conscience about this when we met in later life, until she confessed that all the tales she had told us about tiger-shoots had been her own invention to counter our teasing.

The school was run by three sisters, all unmarried, and the head of my house was Miss Patty, the other being Miss Ada and Miss Bea (Beatrice), the eldest and the Headmistress. Miss Patty was a slight, nervous woman with a wry smile and questioning eyes; she treated dormitory feasts in the most sensible way, by asking whether we were getting enough to eat, which took the fun out of them. She read the fourth leader from the 'Times' to us every morning. The school was keen on nature study and art. We each had a patch in the garden to cultivate, and pets were encouraged, even ponies. The art mistress, old Miss Williams with her grey bobbed hair and cigarette dangling from her mouth, took us into the fields and country lanes to paint carpets of wild flowers. Some girls came from Wales and even Ireland; one from Argyll brought her own pony. My journey was across London with a 'Universal aunt' to Liverpool Street which was full of the steaming, hissing trains of the Great Eastern Railway, and on my first encounter with it I was violently sick out of the train window in a tunnel filled with smoke.

Once home there were all the family to welcome me, as well as a cat and dog, guinea pigs and rabbits. My mother was concerned about agricultural workers having no unemployment pay, and would make speeches to them standing in a lane, while they listened from behind a hedge, afraid of dismissal if they were caught. She supplied the servants with the *Daily Herald* to read, and tried to teach them to swim, which none of the villagers ever did. My father would have made more of his labour-saving devices, and was experimenting with a 'crystal set' and a huge wireless mast on the house. When Alan Cobham came to Great Yarmouth to give rides in his small open 'plane, Priscilla and I went up with him, over the sea, our hair streaming behind us; and my father designed and made a similar 'plane as a weathercock.

We had farms on both sides of us, and the one from which we got our milk each day belonged to Mr Watson, who had sixteen children, the youngest of whom brought our milk across the meadow between us. Mrs Watson went to church each Sunday with a pony and trap. We used to think of the children in pairs, – Molly and Ellen, Percy and Stanley, Hilda and Nell, Rex and John and so on; some were much older than us but Rex, a handsome boy, was about my age. My mother had brought a maid called Ann over from Ireland with her, who served us as cook, and would never go back to Belfast because she had been so terrified of the rough crossing; instead she married Percy Watson and they bought another small farm in the village where we would go and stay if we were in quarantine for any of the childhood illnesses, and also go for tea with Ann who was one of our dearest friends, who always made us a sponge cake, serving us in her front parlour where hung the picture my mother had given her as a wedding present – *The Age of Innocence*.

We made many expeditions to Lowestoft, to the open-air baths and to the fish market to watch the Scotch fisher-girls who came down in the herring season to gut the fish, busy knitting as they waited for the ships to come in, with their needles tucked under their arms over huge leather aprons; their ruddy faces and Scottish accent fascinated us. To get to the market we took an open-top tram, the brass rails almost touching as they swayed past each other on the hill in the main street.

But my going to boarding school had sad consequences for us; my mother wanted the others to go there too, as day girls, and she also wanted to be nearer her twin sister and my father's favourite brother, Edwin. Also, for her health, she felt she should move. So the cold winds, which stunted the trees and drove the waves to eat away the cliffs, drove us away too. I spent the last night in the little room next to the nursery where I had been after my accident, and where I could hear the sound of the sea. We drove off by car with the dog and the guinea-pigs, leaving behind Olive, Lily, Grace and Ruth with whom we had grown up and gone for comfort in the cosy 'servants hall' behind the green baize door. 'If Manor Close is not sold' I wrote, 'we shall come back next summer holidays. We shall miss everything terribly, especially the sea . . . we *loathe* leaving it and mean to get back here somehow even if we have to wait till we are all grown up and can buy it with our own savings.'

Iona, Gianino and Pat on Wadham Barge – Eights week 1932.

Chapter Two

Oxford and After

The move to Sussex changed our lives. My father missed the sea, which he had been used to watching for ships through his binoculars or a telescope; my mother missed her school committees and her political work, she became a Labour magistrate and joined the Howard league for Penal Reform. Brighton, our nearest large town, with its fine sea-front and historical fantasy – the Royal Pavilion – was far more sophisticated then Great Yarmouth or Lowestoft, and we were only an hour by train from London. My father, also, was not far from his favourite brother, Edwin, who had a large workshop in which he was perfecting a clock to rival Greenwich which is now in the Science Museum in London.

My sisters joined me at the P.N.E.U. school, at first motoring every day in our Austin Seven, driven by our chauffeur gardener, and later being boarders. We all went on to University, three of us to Oxford and the youngest to London; this was unusual for the school, only two other girls seeking and obtaining university places while I was there; one went to Oxford, the other, my best friend – a painter and musician from North Wales – could have gone also to Oxford but chose the Royal Academy School instead.

Under my mother's strong influence I took Politics, Philosophy and Economics (P.P.E.) at Oxford, though I should have been more interested in History or English, but in those days students did not easily change subjects. I gained more from the social life of the University than from the academic, joining several clubs which met in the evenings – the Labour Club, the October Club (Communist), the English Club and the Irish Club. At a 'Social' held by the Labour Club, my friend Pat Wood, from the hostel in which I was living – Springfield St. Mary – and I met two under-graduates, Denis Wright and Basil Cartland, who had come out of curiosity, because they had heard that 'the prettiest girls belong to the Labour Club'; these included at that time, Barbara Betts (Castle) and 'Peter' Spence, the mistress of Bertrand Russell. Another admirer of Pat was Gianino Previtali, an exuberant Italian-American, and from that time we four, or five, called ourselves 'Hell's Angels', from a contemporary film, and in Gianino's Morris Minor car had many escapades, one being to the Newbury races, when Gianino ran down the course with Pat, and landed in a water-jump.

Leaving Oxford with only a Pass Degree I could not get the job I wanted, to work in the Times Book Club in Wigmore Street, London, where only a 'Second' would count. I had an allowance from my father which I could live on without a job, and I decided to go to New York and study commercial art in Parson's School there; it had a branch in Paris, but a favourite cousin (the son of the uncle who had given me books) encouraged me to go to America and gave me introductions there. I was to stay in a women's club, the American Womens Association, and be under the guardianship of friends of my family in the British Consulate, Roger and Constance Stevens; years later Denis was to work under Roger when he, Roger, was Ambassador in Iran. In 1934 they were expecting a child and were enjoying New York; they took me to my first night-club, where the band played 'Smoke gets in your eyes'. They also introduced me to a group of German students, one of whom, John Hertz, I met again in Chicago in 1949; I had completely lost touch with them all, but another, a Count von Felsen, was to embarrass us by turning up in the Athenée Palas Hotel in Bucharest in 1940, where he recognised me and asked me to have coffee with him.

In New York, too, I went to the famous Cotton Club, where white people did not dance but watched the blacks from a balcony. In my room at the A.W.A. I was delighted to find a radio, on which I could hear Groucho Marx and other famous stars. Then at Easter time I took the train down to Charleston, Carolina, and saw the wisteria in bloom on the eighteenth century houses.

Returning to London I joined the Central School of Arts and Crafts in Holborn, and after trying various lodging houses, settled in a studio flat in No. 76 Charlotte Street, with a painter, Thelma Hulbert, whom I met at the 'Central'. The studio at No. 76 had belonged to Constable for fifteen years. The house now belonged to Norah Back, a lady who had a house in Norfolk but had been the mistress of Augustus John, and whose daughter – known as Gwynneth Johnstone – now wanted to study art in London. Gwynneth decorated their rooms in the house with large frescoes. Thelma and I slept and worked in our studio, and let our large, elegant front room to Laurence Whistler, the writer and glass engraver. Charlotte Street still had residents who belonged to the Bloomsbury Group, but the Euston Road School had been opened at the top of the street by Victor Pasmore, Claude Rogers and William Coldstream, and Thelma became the secretary. The two pubs, the Fitzroy Tavern and the Marquess of Granby were still, like the Café Royal, filled mainly with artists in the late mornings and evenings, and the restaurants like Schmidts, Bertorellis, Vianis and the Eiffel Tower were known all over London, especially for their foreign food. Bloomsbury and Chelsea were the two districts where one saw beards, sandals and gypsy-like clothing.

I did not study seriously at the Central, only doing Life drawing under John Farleigh and clay modelling under Skeaping, but I became more and more interested in filming. Thelma and I went frequently to the cinema, she insisting that we sat through both the feature films, the news reels and the cartoons, to get our money's worth. Our favourite actor was Charles Boyer, and our favourite film *Mayerling*. I had read

Film making by Pudovkin, and realised the thrill of cutting and editing, and I edited a film of dancers in Bali by Beryl de Zoete. Her lover, Arthur Waley, was a shadowy figure in her flat, but his brother, who worked for the British Film Institute, gave me a job reviewing films for children in the Bulletin they circulated to cinemas. At home, in Sussex, I filmed the weddings of friends, though no cameras were allowed in the church then, only in the porch. I enjoyed the casual, friendly atmosphere of 'Bohemian' life, but it did not entirely satisfy me, after Oxford.

In 1934 and 1935 I went to Russia, arranged through Intourist, first with a group called Design in Industry, consisting of architects and advertisers, then with actors and journalists to the Moscow Theatre Festival, to see plays, opera, films and the puppet theatre. Nearer home, I went with groups of Oxford friends to Switzerland and Austria for winter-sports. This was by train and cross-channel ferry, joining crowds of enthusiasts with their skis on the 'continental' side of Victoria Station, and ending, sometimes, with a sleigh-ride by moonlight to a remote village such as Ober-gurgl on the Austrian-Italian border. Then, in 1937, I decided to go round the world, through Russia to China and Japan, and then to the United States, to Hollywood, where I would have introductions to film directors, provided again by my cousin. My mother found me a companion for the journey as far as China – Dinah Stock, a W.E.A. lecturer whom she had met teaching in Lewes jail and whose keen desire was to go to India and work with Gandhi. We set off, through Germany and Poland . . .

I wrote

'At Negerolje, the frontier station, Russian soldiers in long heavy trench coats and fur caps were pacing up and down in the snow. It was a very dark night and there was an icy wind. Negerolje is only a small village but the customs house is palatial with "workers of the world unite" written high on the walls all round, in different languages. When the officials had looked at all our books and papers and letters and sealed our camera according to the rule for transit passengers, we waited in the restaurant.

This dim room is unnaturally large for such a small station and, as there is never time to eat, the silent waiters, the glass covered food and the rows of tables all laid for a meal seem quite unreal.

Moscow is one of the quietest cities in the world, even when it is not under snow. In January it snowed lightly every day, slanting at first one way and then another in an indefinite wind. It lay quite firmly in the streets and was not brushed away, but allowed to freeze hard there at nights so that the children skated on it. They skated down to the Kremlin Square to see the big New Year tree, surrounded by coloured stalls and side-shows and covered with yellow electric lights, against a very grey sky. People hurried about in fantastically bulky fur coats and caps . . . family heirlooms from their smells, and because of the high price of fur in the stores.

In the Red Square there was a long slow line, as usual, waiting to pass through the Lenin Mausoleum.

While my companion saw factories and the Parks of Culture and Rest I searched for Russian friends and found them looking older than ever for their age, and thinking only of their children's health and clothing, never of their own, as if they had left their personalities behind with the Revolution. Finding them necessitated a great deal of wandering about, first through the main shopping streets and then along the Pushkin gardens, backwards and forwards in search of the right turning. The shops all seemed very expensive still, even to Russians, and so were cinema and theatre tickets. The big store behind the Bolshoi theatre was crowded with people from top to bottom, many of them peasants in straw boots and sacking gaiters, hung round with fragments of sheepskin.

On the Greek Christmas Day I enquired for the services still held in some of the churches, but always received wrong directions; not intentionally wrong, Russians always try to be helpful and so quite invent things, I think. Of the four churches near the New Moscow Hotel one was an apartment house, another a library, another a public hall and a fourth was closed. All had been restored outside as churches. The last eagle had been removed from the Kremlin towers and a Red star put in its place, but otherwise the city cannot look very different, anyway in the snow, from the Moscow of the nineteenth century.

We went to King Lear performed by the Jewish theatre, exactly the same production and main cast as I had seen over a year before in the Theatre Festival, and to a film commemorating Pushkin, and to *We of Kronstad*. The cinemas do not have continuous performances, and one waits for the next 'house' in a hall with a band playing; besides the big films there is only a short news-reel. In *We of Kronstad* the audience was uncannily apathetic towards both the patriotism and the horrors of war displayed.

The New Moscow Hotel is still cleaned with twig brooms."

Trans-Siberia 1937 (From *Time & Tide* Sept. 1937)

"It is dark when a Trans-Siberian express arrives at the Eastern frontier station of Otpur in Soviet Mongolia, and even if there is a moon, the passenger does not have time, on the short walk along the platform, to accustom his eyes to anything less bright than the lights of the train. To meet armed soldiers on the way is not startling, because there are some on every station, and many on the train itself. This particular one was filled, until the last few days, with 'rabochii sheleznogoroshnik' (railway workers), travelling all the way from Moscow to Sverdlovsk, Chita, Irkutsk and Udinsk. They did not regard themselves as soldiers, but during the journey they wore blue serge breeches and cotton tunics with red stars on the collars, and they left the train in long khaki trench-coats, high leather boots, and little pointed fur caps which look like German helmets.

They chatter in the corridors all day, sometimes whistling to the gramophone records of old jazz songs and Soviet marches which were amplified in each carriage. Or they played chess. most of them ate their own food in their compartments, making tea from water fetched from the various station samovars, and did not appear in the dining-car. They talked to us, not so much asking questions as airing their own knowledge of world geography and politics, and wanting confirmation of it as far as we could give any. Our own position seemed to mystify them. Was my father a Duke, said one, that I could afford such a long journey? But when the train was delayed for three hours because the couplings between the last two carriages had broken, these 'railway workers' strolled about the line in the snow, smoking and chatting, with no suggestion or help to offer. And on the last day when they had all left the train we were almost alone among soldiers, a dozen or more officers who travelled to the frontier from places in Soviet Mongolia. These we did not speak to or understand. Most of them were thick-set, square-headed Mongolians, with inscrutable faces.

There were only five transit passengers, as we all knew very well by that time having met day after day in the dining-car. A Swiss boy was travelling this way to Osaka as it was the quickest route. My companion from England was going to India, I to America, and there were two Chinese gentlemen going to Shanghai. The Swiss boy was only twenty-two and already homesick; he was not much concerned with his surroundings, although being of an engineering turn of mind, he was interested in the technicalities of the journey. He watched the two engines being changed every few hours, and pointed out that it was a pre-war train and so had to go slowly even on the plains, for fear of rattling apart, and he told us the story of the accident on Lake Baikal in the days when the rails were laid across the ice. He was travelling 'first category' and had a large, blue plush compartment, gold embroidered, and shared, strangely enough, with a 'railway worker'.

At Otpur, the temperature was well below freezing point

and we were hurried by a soldier with little ceremony to a small station waiting-room, empty except for one long trestle table, a large stove and two men in plain overcoats who were the only customs officials. They examined all the luggage very thoroughly, but made no remarks and confiscated nothing. The seals which had been put on to cameras on the European border were cut off, and we went back to the train, lying as if it had been abandoned, but there was an occasional splitting, crackling sound; the guards were hacking at the huge icicles which hung in a fringe from the footboards.

After a wait of twenty minutes in one of the plush compartments – in silence and seeing and hearing nobody – the train started suddenly, ran on for a few miles, and we were at Manchouli in Manchukuoan territory, feeling ourselves giants. A tiny Japanese porter came to meet us, swinging a coloured paper lantern to light the track through the snow, and instead of the dim, stuffy waiting-room we were led into a large, clean hall, big enough for a gymnasium and filled with long benches. The contrast between the two stations seemed to be purposely exaggerated by the Japanese. Several tidy porters brought in the luggage, a uniformed official examined it while soldiers stood by. The Russians had said that all Russian papers, books and postcards would be confiscated, which they were. Our cameras were sealed again, and they carried off our English books. We were led upstairs to a small room in which sat, at four desks, four more men, neatly dressed and delicate in manner. We sat on a bench and were called up one by one to answer questions and to fill in forms at great length with details of our families, their means and occupations, how long we wished to stay in Manchukuo and exactly which places we would visit; also, what was our purpose in going there. While the Swiss boy was producing copious credentials prepared by his firm for one of the men, the other three, their short arms folded, sat back in their chairs and gazed intently at my companion and at me; finally they whispered and grimaced to each other behind their hands. An interpreter eventually led us away, intending to accompany us as far as Harbin. We passed the old Russian train still spluttering and hissing, and the old stewards with their cropped heads and worn aprons – young men are not wasted on these jobs – who were rather clumsily tidying their dining-car. Beyond it lay an almost brand-new express, brilliantly lit and polished . . . 'Now you will be comfortable' said the interpreter as we scrambled up.

In our compartment the berths were neatly made up, coloured cotton kimonos lay on them with sandals beside them on the floor. It was 3 a.m. so the interpreter left, explaining where we could find him and we seemed to have the train to ourselves.

It ran very smoothly; all the switches worked, the window would open, and whereas on the Russian train the water was mostly cold, here both taps ran boiling water. We naturally enjoyed these comforts, back to more familiar European standards once more. Yet we could not sleep. It was clear moonlight, and the train crept softly through a wide and supposedly empty valley; but there had been an attack only a few months back, and there were soldiers on guard in each coach. Some had the compartment next to ours and we could hear them pacing about and clattering their swords. At intervals of little more than an hour they would open our door without warning and look round. They were tiny men in large fur caps as tall as busbies. We often found that the train had stopped, but not by any station; it would wait a few minutes and soldiers would get out and walk up and down the line; we could hear them talking under our window and see the tips of their caps and their bayonets passing. Then the train would start again, gently and silently.

Breakfast next morning was served in the dining-car by young Japanese girls, but we missed the two Chinese, who were hoping to get through to Shanghai. They were not there for lunch either, and we never saw them again."

I wrote home . . .

"We arrived in Pekin, surrounded by its high walls – only

the railway station was outside them – and went to stay in the Hotel du Nord, run by a German. We had not brought any introductions with us, so found our own way about, Dinah – with her left-wing sympathies – refusing to take ricksaws because of the sad state of most of the boys pulling them. We saw Shadow Plays, palaces, and a monastery where monks wore saffron yellow . . .

By the Temple of Heaven there is a large notice saying 'HANDS OFF', in the Imperial Throne Room of the Forbidden City it says:–

1. No smoking in the Palace is allowed
2. No confusion is allowed
3. No compare with the things exhibited is allowed
4. No photo or touch to the things exhibited is allowed
5. Care must be taken of the glass of the cases
6. The exhibition is furnished every day and no close is decided on Sunday.

It is impossible to describe it all after a visit of only a fortnight. Its fascination begins at once, from the outside, because it is a high-walled city standing in a desert of flat, open fields, and outside the walls, especially in the Western Hills, there are bandits. Everything inside, especially the oldest and most squalid section – the Tartar city – is so fascinating, and there is so much evidence of artistic sense. All the trading is done in the streets and each seller has such an inventive mind that even if he has only three nuts left, he will arrange them in the most decorative way, in a star or in a circle. And with modern inventions like bi-cycles, instead of a piece of string round the hubs of the wheels to keep them clean they have rings of woollen flowers, and their riders carry paper lanterns instead of lamps. Temples are all the more lovely for being deserted, because ten years of falling into dis-repair have mellowed their blue and gold walls. The throne room in the Forbidden City is as high as the nave of a Cathedral and the carved ceiling can only be seen dimly, but gold dragons twist up the huge pillars which have neither base nor capital; right at the top you can see their eyes gleaming, made of peacock feathers.

Out in the marble courtyards there are weird stone animals and nightingale cages. The nightingale was a favourite bird of the Emperors but now there do not seem to be many birds, though once inside the walls of the Forbidden City none of the clanging and shouting in the streets outside can be heard. The strangest thing about the Buddhas in the temples is that they sit inside towers with very little space round them and so appear very tall."

On the train from Pekin to Mukden, on my way to Japan, I met some missionaries. They could all speak Chinese. Dr and Mrs . . . had worked in Manchuria for thirty-six years and answered all my questions about it. As to bandits, the Doctor had encountered some in the mountains during his journeys by cart to different outposts, but when he mentioned his predecessor, a very well-known missionary, they had not harmed him. His wife said that he had seldom much money on him to lose but she always hoped especially that they would not take his overcoat so that he would die of cold.

During our meals together on the train they said that one must always peel apples in China. They were sorry for me travelling alone, having left Dinah in Pekin, and suggested we should all spend the evening together in Mukden as our trains would both probably leave about eleven o'clock. So we had dinner in the grill-room at the Yamato Hotel after an exhausting encounter with railway officials over sleeper tickets. I could not get one and the missionaries were worried about it.

After dinner we saw *San Francisco* in quite a large cinema but it was very hot inside and there was a bad smell as we were near the cloakrooms, so that after the noise too and the flickering of the earthquake and fire I could not help going outside for some air. Mrs . . . soon hurried out very kindly and brooded again on the long journey ahead of me, and then we both went back again to see the repentance of the hero, on his knees on a hill above the smoking ruins. A very Japanese film followed, and the programme ended at ten-thirty with the playing of *Auld Lang Syne*.

We had to wait till midnight on the station, and had some tea and biscuits and jam. The main waiting-room was large, but almost full of Chinese peasant families, mostly ragged and tired, squatting in circles on their coloured cotton bundles. Russian peasants camp on their stations in the same way waiting days for trains, but these people were just being turned out of Manchuria by the Japanese, the missionaries said, though they had no idea what provision was being made for them. If Europeans go away singly and wait among Easterners an hour passes quickly and calmly, but this one seemed to drag as a thousand little arrangements were vigorously discussed. The whole evening was worthwhile for one thing, however; we took a droshki from the cinema to the station in the snow, and as it was so cold the discussion of tickets was postponed while we muffled up our mouths. The silence was wonderful; we might have been any sort of people, going anywhere."

Crossing the pacific in a Japanese ship, the *Chichibu Maru*, because of a dock strike in San Francisco, we stopped in Honolulu beside a British cruise liner. I went aboard to study the passenger list and found that my Uncle James and his wife were on it; he had become the first Prime Minister of Northern Ireland, and was taking this cruise to avoid the embarrassment of a divorce in the family. But they were ashore and we never met.

From the Figueroa Hotel in Los Angeles, I wrote to Denis:–

The success of this visit really depends on whether I find the film people to whom I have introductions . . . sitting in trains and steamers I have evolved film plans which I shall not tell you because you have heard so many . . . Japan was

24

Fancy dress in the Chichibu Maru – 1937.
Iona in front in Coolie hat

an extraordinary experience, what a complete ritual their life still is, especially the women, none of them looked worried and they all have such delicate and calm manners. At first it struck me as absurd that they don't even allow skating in pairs, much less any ball-room dancing, and Europeans have to get licences for dancing and keep to themselves too, but soon I liked them, compared to the Americans. There were seven nationalities on board my ship – Dutch (from Java), French, German, American, Hungarian, English and Japanese. There were fourteen missionaries, mostly from India. I have never encountered such a lot before, and they soon swarmed all over me. I was doing some sewing on deck and they paraded past saying, "Busy little maid! Oh my how she works," etc. There are two at my table and I hear all about their hospitals and schools. When there is a nice sunset they trip about the deck saying, "My, what a beautiful world!" In contrast there was an American basketball team on board who spent most of the time in the bar, and when the missionaries tried to admonish them they only shouted out, "here comes a missionary we haven't toasted!"

In Hollywood I used my introduction to the film directors, Leo McCarey and Norman McLeod, who showed me over the whole set of Universal Pictures, covering about one hundred acres and where they were making nine pictures simultaneously. There were German, French and American villages . . . piles of dead bodies for the latest Remarque film, the lower half of Rheims or Chartres cathedral, also the remains of the *Showboat* boat, a Chinese temple and the hall and stairs from *My Man Godfrey*.

I then took the Santa Fe-railway to the East coast, visited Gianino Previtali in the lovely southern city of Charlottesville, Virginia, and went home on the Italian liner, *Rex*.

In 1939 I found work in the library of Gaumont-British Films in Shepherds Bush, which might have led to what I wanted, to be a 'continuity girl' on a film set; I enjoyed searching for shots of Nelson's column, or Buckingham Palace, for directors who did not want to have to take them again. But then came the War, and the studios were closed down. Thelma and I had taken a cottage in the country, to which we could invite friends, as a refuge; we found that we were known locally, in the village, as 'them in the woods'.

On September 3rd, 1939 I wrote:–

"Set out from the cottage this morning meaning to 'phone home, then walk to Penn and enquire for Diana and Rab. No call possible and Penn is five miles. Decide to go to London. Catch bus and train quite easily and man in train says war is declared and there has already been a raid on London. I wonder whether to get out halfway and go back but I feel it cannot be right about the raid. A mother and small girl got in, going back to Hammersmith because the child can't stand evacuation. Mother quite resigned, says she has eleven children, one dying in hospital in south London; this one has cried all night for her father.

Several other mothers also bringing children back – when we reach London they all talk as they pass on the platform saying what a rotten business evacuation was – couldn't stand leaving home, sooner be killed there than away. I saw a mother with a little girl going off on the Met, bursting paper bags all their luggage. I went by bus to Russell Court. No sign of Denis. Walked to Charlotte Street. Met no-one I knew. Collect a few things from the flat, get a coffee at Buhlers. Go to station again at 4 o'clock. Train at 5.15. Ring up home with some trouble. A lot of people walking about in gas masks; not many soldiers. Posters just say "WAR official". In a café I am not allowed a glass of milk. Wretched exhausted children still going to the station. A good many War Police in blue helmets, more notices of shelters and First Aid, more sandbags than two days ago. Quite a lot of buses still running. Taxes available as usual. In the train there is a tough young mother with noisy handsome small girl who says she eats matches and string and mud and sticks and sand; when she screams the mother says 'stop or I'll put on your gas mask' 'that'll frighten her all right' she says to me . . .

September 5th. Do not particularly notice 'State of War', bright day, very hot in afternoon. I catch the same bus and train to London and find it the same as Sunday except for a few more sandbags. Not nearly as many people about as on weekdays usually. Thwarted at various points, Piccadilly Underground closed when I want to leave my case there and Brasserie Universelle menu written in pencil on slip of paper and much depleted. People often amusing all with little gas mask boxes banging on their backs, crooked on the end of bits of string. Especially city men, look as if they have lunch boxes. Woman in bus wants to sit near the door, which is next to me, and tells me of old lady having a fit at the 2.30 a.m. air raid rehearsal on Monday, which I am glad I missed. All barrage balloons are up like silver fish in the sky. I call at the flat, it is apparently inhabited by someone. Several 'locals' are wandering about Charlotte Street, not yet evacuated. Victoria Station much the same, a few soldiers wandering about. For twenty-nine minutes out of thirty I find I don't remember the war. Telephoning is easy. War Police are ugly. At the Palace men are in khaki instead of the red and black sentries. Flower and fruit barrows are in the streets as usual. Shops are open though their windows are cross-crossed with brown paper strips. Cinemas are shut. I ring the British Film Institute and find there will be no trade shows till cinemas are open again.

Going home to Sussex in the train there is less feeling of war then ever, in fact none at all – because I know the country and it looks just the same; going to the cottage I do not know it so it *might* have been different."

On leaving Oxford Denis had got a job in advertising. We saw each other from time to time as he enjoyed the atmosphere of Charlotte Street, dances at the Central School of Art, and the annual Chelsea Arts Ball etc. In 1939 we got engaged but in August he went off alone on holiday to Roumania – a long standing desire of his – passing through Berlin where he stayed with German friends. When he reached the Black Sea port of Constanța with an introduction to Tony Kendall, the British Consul there, war seemed imminent. Kendall urged him not to cut short his holiday as, in the event of war, he could do useful, and urgent, work in the Consulate. So, after exchanges between the Legation in Bucharest, the Foreign Office, and Gallahers Ltd (his employers) he became a temporary member of H.M. Consular Service.

When I heard this I decided to join him. I crossed the Channel in an almost empty boat on Friday the thirteenth of October, and took the Orient Express from Paris to Bucharest.

It was many years before I reached Colorado, and sent postcards home to my sisters . . .

Denis in the flat, Constanţa

Chapter Three

Black Sea Bride

The weather was bright and sunny and very windy on most days, a strong, fresh sea breeze, and the Consulate building at Constanţa in which we were staying creaked and rattled all the time. There was a Spanish-style balcony running round the upper floor with several rooms leading out onto it, the doors of which were always banging. The windows were double and had bars and shutters as well; all was a bit dilapidated, but the sound of the sea was loud at night and drowned all others.

We had very nice food; fresh fish from the sea and the Danube, a lot of meat, all sorts of vegetables, and chicken and eggs. All food came from open street markets, where it was necessary to bargain.

Our first problem was to find a flat, and then to arrange for our marriage; as Kendall, the Consul in Constanţa, had no marriage licence, I had to go by car to Galatz, on the Danube, to put up the bans, though no-one would be likely to contest them there. It was a three-hour journey each way, in a car which had been lent to Kendall by a Roumanian who did not want to have it confiscated in war time, and the driver and I were stopped in remote villages, suspected of being Poles, as the refugee camps were nearby. After crossing the Danube by ferry we went on foot to the Consulate, and then had to start back immediately to reach Constanţa by nightfall. Kendall and his Bulgarian wife, Mila, very kindly let us stay in the Consulate until we could find a flat, and Mila introduced me to the market, the shops, and the problems of housekeeping. For household linen, I had to buy material and make sheets, pillow cases, and even pillows, on her sewing-machine and we visited country markets in nearby villages where chicken feathers could be bought, but the usual stuffing for mattresses was straw, while quilts were made of wool covered with brightly coloured silk.

We found a flat in the main square of the town, the Piaţa Ovidiu. This was a large open space, with cafés and shops on one side and the Primaria, or Town Hall, on the other. In the centre was a graceful statue of Ovid who had spent eight years of exile here, from the year A.D. 8. Constanţa was a mixed population of Roumanians, Greeks, Bulgars, Turks, Italians, Armenians and Jews, mostly engaged in shipping, and the evening 'corso' through the Square, for eight months of the year, was a colourful sight, most of the populace strolling up and down beneath our windows, enjoying the cool of the day.

After our wedding, to which the local British colony of Galatz were invited, none of whom we knew, but who made a friendly group round us as the consul-general, resplendent in his uniform, faced us across a table covered in the Union Jack, we had a short honeymoon in the mountains of Transylvania, staying our first night in the Palace Hotel at Sinaia, which owing to the very favourable rate of exchange was not expensive, and we could join the crowds in the Casino at night.

We had taken a very slow train from Galatz to Buzau, where the Kendall's car was waiting to drive us to Sinaia, a summer resort rather like Grindelwald, but quite deserted now. The weather was perfect and we drove up to a mountain restaurant which was closed but was worth seeing because of the view. In the evening we went to the Casino, and though the town had seemed empty, here there were crowds. Denis bought a flat check cap, and wore a bow-tie, looking very un-Roumanian. We were usually taken for Polish refugees. There were always a great many soldiers about, but they were friendly. At the next place – Brasov – there was a Wild West

Black Sea Bride

British Consulate – Constanţa

Piaţa Ovidiu, Constanţa

33

film showing called 'Melody of the Plains' ('Banda din Far West') but we did not see it because it was at 11 a.m. Then in Fagaraş there was a cinema showing 'Katia' which we decided to see while our stove was being lit. They burn oak and lime here, just using pine-wood to start off the fire, with its resin, (but they are all difficult to cook on, needing constant stoking). Of course the big terra-cotta stoves stay hot for ten or twelve hours after having a fire in them for only one hour, but they are only for heating. We started buying furniture for our flat on our return, finding that a dressing-table cost the equivalent of seven-and-sixpence, the same price, I noted, as a pound of imported China tea.

I wrote home . . .

"Our furniture should have arrived yesterday afternoon in the flat and I waited for it, mostly in the dark because the electricity is not turned on yet. However it did not come. Then at 7.30 this morning the office boy arrived to say that he had seen it all outside our flat, so I went there and found one old peasant and two boys of about sixteen and one about seven who were not at all skilled at carrying furniture; they took it on their heads and so could not see where they were going or where the corners were catching.

Last night Lady Hoare, wife of our Minister in Bucharest, arrived to stay the night at the Consulate and then to drive with K. to see the Polish soldiers who were interned in an out of the way village and reported to be in a very bad condition. (Her husband had served in Poland). She came by train and Denis and K. met her at four o'clock, with a representative of the Constanţa Red Cross who presented her with a large bunch of chrysanthemums; when she reached the Consulate Mrs K. thought they were for her. Lady H. wore three pullovers, all of different lengths and colours. She is also a relief worker and was one in the last war. She is also a pilot. She kept talking about propellors and compasses, and I could not think why until I was told. In the village there are about five thousand Poles

34

quartered in ramshackle camps; the Red Cross has so far not reached them, many hundreds have malaria and dysentry, and only five nurses, three priests and three doctors are looking after them, many of them with no blankets and lying on bare earth. Lady H. has raised a tremendous outcry about it, and has arranged for oxygen to be sent by taxi for one pneumonia case. As to the linen you have sent us we are still waiting and now Denis thinks we shall have to pay after all – 6000 lei, which is three pounds, ten shillings; it is worth it to have it and we only hope it will not be stolen at the last minute. According to British Captains this is the most corrupt port in the Near East. They have regularly to give the harbour authorities whisky, jam, cigarettes, silk, cigars and fruit until they get any attention."

We moved into the flat and found it well-heated by the tiled stoves which are traditional in the Balkans, and also by radiators and double windows to keep out the icy winds which swept the town in winter. Ovid had written in his 'Tristia' that "With skins and stitched breeches they keep out the evils of the cold: of the whole body only the face is exposed. Often the hair tinkles with hanging ice and their beards glisten white with the mantle of frost. Exposed wine stands upright retaining the shape of the jar and they drink, not draughts of wine, but fragments." In December I watched from our windows as people clung to lamp-posts and small boys ran a short distance, then crouched down on their heels to get their breath. The main Orthodox church was in a street nearby, and funeral processions would pass, the huge hearse piled with flowers, the horse covered in black trappings which would flap in the wind, while the attendant mourners would struggle with trays of food and gifts for the soul of the dead person, dressed themselves in black costumes with knee-breeches and buckled shoes.

We had a nice time up at Galatz for the New Year, though the snow there made the train late, and leaving Constanţa at 10 p.m. we did not arrive until a quarter to four in the morning.

We went by sleigh to the hotel, the sleigh had bells and ribbons for the New Year. The coachmen wear enormous padded coats, tightly belted, with full skirts. We were to stay with the Archbolds, shipping people, their maid brought their key round and said that they were ski-ing. They lent us skates in the afternoon, to skate on a frozen tennis court, which was fun, and then there was a fancy-dress party at nine-o'clock. A Greek lady in Constanţa had lent me a flower-seller's costume, quite pretty, and Denis wore a sailor's suit. It was my idea that he should get one from the Naval school, and it looked nice and was comfortable. There were about thirty guests and we were up till 3 a.m. The Archbolds made us very comfortable and lent us several books and old copies of 'Punch'. They had copies of the 'Illustrated London News' of 1878 and Denis found in it long articles and pictures about my great grandfather, Sir George Nares, and his Arctic exploration.

While shopping for our household equipment I would have difficulty in carrying it, but it was the custom for small boys to carry a customer's purchases, and ladies were not meant to do it themselves. All shops worked on the apprentice system, with children who would climb on to the high shelves, or hold hairpins and basins of water in the hairdressers. In barbers' shops Denis would often see army officers having their nails manicured. In winter they wore frogged, waisted jackets, high boots and astrakhan caps, and were an elegant sight when driving in sleighs in Bucharest, where the streets were often deep in snow.

With our flat we had taken on a gypsy-like servant-girl, called Maiora, who worked for another tenant in the building, Madame Isoviç, an old Jewish lady who was very apprehensive, like all Jews, of German influence in Roumania and who dreamed of escape to Turkey and Palestine. She sold us one or two of her possessions, including a large feather eiderdown*, and she would ask me to tea in her over-heated sitting-room to talk of the war over a cup of tea and the Roumanian jam 'dulceaţa'.

*We still use it today.

Her husband was Paramount representative in Berlin, but is dead now. She married a Roumanian in order to get to Roumania, but does not live with him. She is small and old, but bright, with painted nails and lipstick, also dyed red hair. Everything in her flat is spotlessly clean, but it's the same with all the maids, she says – 'minciuna, minciuna (lies)' and 'sa faces hocus-pocus'. "Maiora, sti se lucraz, aber nu vrea" (knows how to work but does not want to). We did not find Maiora lazy. She cooked and cleaned for us, working bare-footed, with a handkerchief tied on her head, and when we had guests she would wear the small muslin apron I had given her. She scrubbed the parquet floor with wire wool every few months, and then re-polished it.

She is strong – she can undo a waste pipe if it needs cleaning and saves us sending for Stefan, the man-of-all-work who signs himself 'Calorifer'* if he leaves a note about anything.

But Maiora, I see, has finished up the Lyle's Golden Syrup I got in Bucharest for my breakfast, after I remarked to Denis that it would just last until tomorrow. When I suggest a new thing to eat she always says 'Nu stiu, N'am mancat, Niciodata' (I don't know. I haven't eaten it. Never.) There are a lot of vegetables in the market, and fish, but meat is not good, there are now two 'meatless' days a week, Wednesdays and Fridays. Her husband came back from the Transylvanian front last night. When he is home he is a nuisance to us as she shares our food with him if she has not got enough for them both; she supplements from our cupboard, also she does a bit of cooking on our gas, boiling him a kilo of milk, or frying a chicken. The system of husbands living in maids rooms is odd.

Maiora arrived this morning with a live chicken which she put on the kitchen floor. I had ordered chicken soup for lunch. It is quite a common thing here to see a maid in the street with a hen and a knife, stopping a passer-by to ask them to kill it for her, which they do in the gutter; usually it

*Radiator.

37

is a business man on his way home from work. If you buy dead, plucked hens, they are hardly ever fresh.

There is such a wind today, also it is slippery with frozen snow, so that you cannot cross to the open side of the square by the harbour. I looked out of our window, when there was a sudden gust, and saw a man clinging to a lamp-post, and schoolboys first running into the wind, then turning their backs and crouching down on their heels to rest. The lamp-posts are swaying, and all the shop signs too; they will get carried away soon, after crashing backwards and forwards and whirling round on the sticks they hang on. When Mrs Kendall meets the wind at a corner she cries, "Ah, my hat, it will fly!"

She has been telling us about the English governesses she has had for her daughter, Cecilia. One was Irish and very short-sighted. Cecilia stole her glasses so that she was not able to see what she was eating, and she tried to cut up and eat a cork. When something caught fire in the Consulate, and although Mrs K. said they could easily put it out, she rushed to the police-station where she let out a dangerous prisoner from his cell by mistake, as she could not see and opened the wrong door. The prisoner shook hands with her and thanked her very much and disappeared before the warder woke up; when he did he was so furious with Miss O'Mara that he kicked her and broke two of her ribs, so that Mrs K. had to nurse her for six weeks.

We are going to see Cecilia tomorrow, probably, in Galatz where she is in a Convent School. We have to take her an eider-down which it has taken a shop two months to recover, and Mrs K. says it is so heavy that they must have stolen the down and put in wool.

She bought a turkey the other day and it is kept in the cellar where it makes an awful noise. 'It cries' she says, 'because it want friend'.

There was a cavalry regiment quartered near Constanţa, and a Naval School on the sea front whose cadets would march through the street. The main social events for the winter consisted of *thés dansants* or *ceai cu prelungire* which would go on into the early hours of the morning with dancing and card-playing. Naval and Army officers would come in uniform, as would the captain of the port, and the women were smart in black, vying with each other with the jewellery their husbands had bought them. With their dark hair and olive skins, they appeared to us very exotic and sophisticated compared to women in England though their world was a narrow one. The Roumanian family Marcoviç, owners of the small Hotel Francez made themselves the centre of a cosmopolitan group. Madame Marcoviç was French, and her husband a retired Roumanian General. With their three daughters, France, Arlette and Toinon, they would attend the 'thés dansants' and together with a pretty young Roumanian woman married to a Belgian banker, the Polish consul and his wife, the French consul, the Kendalls and ourselves, we would discuss the war situation in-between dances and during the buffet supper which ended the proceedings. The Marcoviç girls were gay and attractive and did not lack partners, though France, over-romantic, was always looking for an ideal husband and was bored with her own countrymen. Madame Hubinon, recently happily married, would tell her . . . "marriage is not all romance, as you think . . . c'est un travail".

Denis was learning Roumanian while giving English lessons at the Anglo-Roumanian Society, a group started by the British Council. He also taught English to the children of one of the rich Greek shipping merchants. In all these contacts he could keep in touch with what was happening in the town, while he and Kendall paid occasional visits to Bucharest, and mysterious visitors from our Legation there came down to the consulate.

The ineffective Roumanian government was coming more and more under German influence and the Allies were planning to sabotage their efforts. Mila and I were surprised one day by the arrival of seventeen 'merchant seamen' on board the Roumanian passenger ship, the 'Transylvania' from Egypt, mostly young boys, who stopped to have tea in the consulate hall where we lit a big log fire to cheer them. They were to man barges loaded with explosives, which would blow up the Iron Gates on the Danube and block German shipping, but only two weeks later they were being hastily deported, when the Germans had urged the Roumanians to search their barges and arrest them.

Mila was particularly relieved when Denis' appointment as vice-consul was confirmed. Tony Kendall had a lively imagination and would dramatise every situation, so that when events of this nature occurred he would become excitable and nervous. "What he make?", she would say to me, as she always translated literally from the French, which they spoke together. "He tell me, burn these boys' coats, burn the caps, we give them plain cloths. How I burn caps in my oven? I not burn, I cut off buttons and I sell them . . ." One of the mysterious visitors brought a limpet bomb to Denis and Tony, in case it was needed to blow up a ship, and they decided to try it on the side of the bath, when Mila thought she would take one. Tony's efforts to keep her out of the bathroom were much more complicated than the real explanation would have been; Mila was a practical person herself and luckily took things calmly.

Spring came suddenly in April, when we could open the windows of the flat and put pots of flowers on the sills. The air became fresh and sweet and all the smells in the town, in the market and in the harbour, became stronger. In the evenings there was a rustle of footsteps in the square and the murmur of voices from the 'corso'. The cafés put out their tables and chairs on the pavements; officers immediately dropped into them. There was a general inertia about the army, as German power increased. Floods came at this time and the road to Bucharest was cut. Each spring the ice floated down the Danube and piled against the banks, crushing the small boats of the peasants and sometimes carrying men and animals out to sea. But the coming of the better weather made the Roumanians fear invasion.

Outwardly, life in Constanţa seemed normal, and in May the long beach at Mamaia, five miles outside the town, was open for swimming, holiday-makers coming down as usual from Bucharest to stay in the large Rex Hotel on the beach, though the Palace of the King next door remained unopened. Residents of Constanţa came out by private car, as the road was bad and there were few buses; we availed ourselves of the Kendall's car and swam and sunbathed on the beach while they sat with friends on the hotel terrace. The Marcoviç family did not possess a car, and in any case the girls did not bathe. There was something provincial about them compared to the smart visitors from Bucharest, and their parents would not have allowed them to go unchaperoned. At night the terrace would be gay with coloured lights, and food was good and plentiful.

Then in May, came the fall of France, which more than anything affected the morale of the Roumanians, they were stunned. The culture of the upper classes had come from France, the language and customs of the country had a Latin background. Now too, the Germans would look eastwards. Italy entered the war, and Russia demanded Bessarabia. This would be followed, by demands from Hungary and Bulgaria. A furious army officer whom we knew, tore off his decorations in front of us. Maiora's husband was in Transylvania, but no fight would be put up there against Hungary. She received a letter from him which another servant translated for her as she could not read; she listened and then returned to polishing the floor... "foarte frumoasa parquet", she remarked (beautiful parquet). Her husband was doing his military service, and every month she gave part of her wages to an officer in Constanţa in order to buy his way out of the army as soon as possible, though they had no home, besides the small room she lived in at the top of our building.

June 1940

"It is another holiday today. A sunny morning, and a procession beginning with school-children. Later the sailor's band, pretty in the sun, with children running in front and the dogs running in and out of the leaders' feet, and much clashing of cymbals. All of them collected outside the Orthodox church and waited there whilst the Mayor went in for a service. Various batches of school-children continued to pass by, singing. After an hour or so they return, the procedure exactly reversed.

Last night it was wet, with thunder. Some soldiers marched by, in the street beside our flat, in tin helmets which shone in the wet. They were all equipped with heavy packs, and looked as if they had come a long way. Italy declared war yesterday. It is getting hot, so that sometimes one keeps windows and balcony doors shut to keep it out. The sun rises early and from nine until two o'clock are the hottest hours. There is nothing outwardly wrong with Constanţa still, in spite of the war spreading, and so near. Only there is no fruit because it comes from Greece and Italy, and there are no more ships. Grapefruit is finished and lemons are sixteen lei; they used to be three lei. At night there is no light, or very little. People are expected not to show any though it is not well controlled. It does not matter much in the bright moonlight or starlight, and simply makes the town look more mysterious. Cabarets have been stopped for several days, as a form of mourning for the loss of Bessarabia to the Russians, and yesterday several of the girls left with piles of luggage for the station, from the Elite Hotel, next door to us, where they stay.

We dined at the Mamaia beach with the Kendalls and Hazell. Hazell was giving his own farewell party, which he did in a most business-like manner. Cecilia Kendall ate a plate of boiled potatoes, which she ordered very precisely for herself, and then announced that she would go back to the car. Kendall took her home as she was tired, and she said to him on the way, "You know, I don't think I am old enough yet to go out to dinner with you". Mrs Kendall was in good form, ready to take up anybody on a word and twist it, in her broken-English – "Likeness? Oh, I think you say 'Nightdress'."

M. Mouillé, the French consul who made his home in the Hotel Francez, decided to follow Pétain, and refused to allow some French naval ratings who were being repatriated to travel on a British ship. He appeared to have grown old almost in one night. M. Hubinon too, decided he must go back immediately to fight in Belgium; he left with his wife and was killed soon after. Communications were cut across Europe, and Roumania ordered general mobilisation. A black-out was imposed in Constanṭa and the merchant fleet was ordered to go to Galatz in case of a Russian invasion.

Food became short, with the loss of shipping from Europe, and two 'meatless' days a week were imposed, though Roumanians were suspicious that the meat was going to Germany. We continued to swim at the beach, to play tennis, and sometimes to join the proprietors of our flat on their yacht, while once a week we joined our friends on the little terrace of the Hotel Francez. France, who was learning English, practised it on us, but she was depressed at the difficulties in realising her ideal, to marry an Englishman. Arlette was an extrovert, ready to laugh and joke like her mother; Toinon the schoolgirl, came arm-in-arm with others girls in their black frocks with white collars, followed at a discreet distance by boys from the Naval School. In August they gave a dance at the hotel to which we were invited with twenty other people, including several of the naval cadets. Mme Marcoviç, dressed informally in a cotton frock and tennis shoes, with a wisp of muslin binding up her reddish hair, finished a game of cards with her husband and served some wine, slapping all the time at mosquitoes. Some of the guests played ping-pong while the rest danced to the gramophone, to the tune of 'Jeepers, creepers' or 'Si, si si' alternately being almost all the records they had, or to the band of the Dorchester Hotel in London on the radio. It had been a wet, thundery day and the rain had come through the roof at several places making the floor sticky to dance on. 'Madame' sat in a deck-chair over one of the pools, with her dog 'Pousse' beside her. Arlette looked fresh in pale blue linen, with bright geranium lipstick. Toinon was quieter than usual because her sailor 'sweetheart' was ill, France was demonstrative with arms and hands, tapping a cigarette or fingering her brooch, glum to begin with, but unlike Toinon whose silence was seriousness, she soon started chattering . . . *Monsieur Wright . . . comment est ce que on dit en Anglais . . .*

M. Mouillé was soon to leave the hotel and return to France. He left without saying goodbye to his old friends, and to the servants he gave some old panes of glass which had fallen out of his window, a piece of a wireless aerial, and some copies of 'L'Illustration', saying in each case, *Vous pouvez les vendre.* There was little work for consulates as shipping had been reduced to a few Greek and Turkish boats. Denis continued to study Roumanian but he and Kendall decided to close the Anglo-Roumanian Institute as pupils dwindled to a few Roumanians and Jews who wanted to go to Palestine.

Bulgaria annexed the Dobrugea and with the exchange of population which took place Turks could be seen in the Constanţa market, the women wearing their national dress of trousers and flowered cotton blouses, as they crouched on their heels with their children eating large, pale yellow melons which were then in season. After the loss of their provinces rioting took place in the larger towns which remained, and the 'Iron Guard' under Premier Antonescu made a show of stopping it with German help. One evening, sitting in a café with some English friends from Bucharest, we heard the sound of shooting nearby and of machine-gun fire from the direction of the port. Across the road the main post office was being attacked. People rushed into the restaurant for cover, and soldiers who had been dining there rushed out. At first we were told it was an attack by the Russians who had landed, then that it was the army attacking the navy. It was not until midnight that a group of sailors arrived and searched us for arms. When Denis asked for a safe conduct to the consulate, he was told that because of fighting in the port we must spend the night in a hotel, and together with our friends we were marched up the street with our hands above our heads, to the 'Carlton' which happened to be the one in which they were staying. It was estimated that at least twenty-five people had been shot by the 'Iron Guard', but with the abdication of King Carol the next day in favour of his son Michael, who became a German protégé, they were pardoned, and those who had lost their lives defending the town against them, as they thought, were buried without ceremony, their coffins carried on old horse-drawn carriages.

September 1940

The Roumanians to-day are behaving in an extraordinary manner. They have had a large funeral of three Iron Guardists who were shot here and have been lying in state. People went to the church all day, yesterday, and this afternoon crowds went there, the whole town it seemed, passing through the square, and at three-thirty an enormous cortège appeared, with a mob pressing behind it, and behind *them* a hundred or more Guardists marching in their new green shirts, made legal to-day. The common soldiers and sailors who were killed, in shooting all through the town two days ago, (in which we also were involved as we got caught in a restaurant near the post office which was one of the centres of trouble) were given no funeral, their coffins being carried through back streets by droshkis, and followed only by their families. But in the crowd to-day there were many staring peasants, and few soldiers and naval officers, since they were ashamed to change their allegiance to quickly.

Dogs ran down the street to the church, stray dogs, as if they knew what was there and had the definite intention of going. Then, half an hour after this slow, sentimental procession, with priests and a droning choir, the huge hearse piled high with wreaths and pulled by green ropes by green-clad youths – a naval band had gone by playing a loud, gay march, with cymbals and drums and led by smart officers and men carrying banners; it must be part of a welcome to King Michael, who has taken over the throne from his father to-day, but it is startlingly gay, so soon on the track of the other.

Evacuees arrive now, British from Bucharest and Galatz,

45

because of the unsettled state of affairs and the growing German power in the country. They stay in the 'Carlton', the only modern hotel, until they can get a passage on a ship to Istanbul, or in the 'Francez'. It is down by the little yacht harbour, with a terrace on top of the cliff, where we often go for a drink. The French Consul lives there, who is old and has left his wife behind in France, as she is an ardent Catholic and insisted on going to church every day, also refused to let him smoke. One of his daughters nearly died, and said she would be a nun if she recovered, which she now is. Mouillé is a dapper little man with a quick wit, but bone lazy. He loves to sit chatting with the three girls at the 'Francez', and plays cards with the General while a (French) refugee from Poland runs the French Consulate alone. Yesterday twelve nuns arrived as evacuees. Mouillé had to 'entertain' them. He was seen leading them to church. The day passed slowly, until at last they were shepherded onto a steamer for Egypt.

K. had a scheme two days ago of defending the Consulate against siege, telling Denis that, since Bucharest seemed to neglect the urgency of the situation, we must take it all into our own hands and summon all the colony to camp in the Consulate. Denis did not agree that anyone would particularly want to besiege it now, and reminded him of the 'Hanne', a U.K. Registered ship which is being kept here for evacuation. K. who had only been talking of it a short time ago, said "My God, yes, I had forgotten 'The Hanne' " and swerved off in another direction of thought. He was later determined that we were completely isolated here, and could not connect with Galatz and the Consul-General, but when the office put through a call they got an answer in ten minutes and then K. did not know what to say.

Miss Lowe, secretary to the oil company, Stella Romana, is staying with us for a week, our first house-guest; she has brought with her some of her employer's furniture, including his radio, some good sherry and vermouth, and a sewing-machine.

The K's are back from a motoring holiday, a few days ago,

and Mila is still tired from the bumping. Last night at dinner she recovered. A cross-eyed man had come into the Consulate, whom she described as 'Look you and see me'. Cissy had been playing Miss Lowe's employer's piano, now stored in the consulate, and she was annoyed and said – "I make he nicely, I see she don't continuer." She always speaks of making people nicely, for some reason, when she wants to scold them.

Mrs Watson a ship's captain's wife, has at last departed, not a great loss to the community, but she has at least left me some cork mats which will be useful, and which we are unable to buy here.

The 'Alcazar' still plays at night, but the 'Luther Bar' has closed. The smaller night clubs continue with local girls, but the slightly better trained ones from Hungary have all left or ceased to come. One, Lola, a singer remains, a powerful middle-aged lady, red-haired and good natured. Her songs, the same she has sung for a year or more now, are the only entertainment offered, beside the band for dancing, at the 'Alcazar'. Every night, since it is just across the square, her high notes float in through our window, a wild lullaby.

Soon after this, some English engineers were arrested in the Ploesti oilfields; they were imprisoned and it was said they were being tortured. The Legation decided on a general evacuation for British subjects, the consulate was to be ready to close at forty-eight hours notice after they had passed through. Denis was to go up to Bucharest to work in the Legation, and we decided that I should go to Istanbul with the general evacuation, to wait there until the Legation finally had to leave, as no one doubted that it would. We gave up our flat and Denis moved to the consulate. Before leaving for Bucharest he saw Mme Marcoviç who had had orders from the German consulate to register her accommodation with them for future use.

Passing through Constanţa when relations between Britain and Roumania were broken off in February 1941, Denis saw the Marcoviçs again. Constanţa was like a German town; there were German soldiers everywhere, marching and singing their war songs. The Piaţa Ovidiu was a vast parking space for German lorries, and the Hotel Francez a German barracks with sixty Germans in occupation. The Marcoviç family, sad and lonely, were touched that he had come to say goodbye. The history of their little hotel was like that of Roumania itself, with good people, trusting in the Allies, swamped by German power. We heard that the family moved to Bucharest where the old people died, and France and Arlette, demoralised by the life in the capital, took lovers. When they were arrested under the communist regime for their contacts with foreigners, they were confronted by their lovers in court, only to find "they" were the same man. They were freed eventually and Arlette married, as did her sister Toinon; but France became seriously ill in prison, and died in hospital.

Denis and I, on separate occasions, sailed to Istanbul, arriving there in the early morning mists, when a turn of the Bosphorus showed all the mosques, palaces and castles in a golden haze, one of the most beautiful sights in the world.

At the beginning of 1941 hotels in Istanbul were filled with British subjects evacuated from the Balkans. Polish soldiers who had managed to escape from Roumania went to join the army in Britain, Polish civilians went to try their luck in East Africa and Rhodesia. British wives and children were being repatriated by ship round the

Cape and I put my name on the waiting list, as Denis had been offered the post of Consul at Trebizond on the Black Sea but thought he should go there alone as it was possible Turkey too might be soon swept into the war. While waiting in Istanbul for my passage and before his arrival from Bucharest, I was given work at the British Embassy, the imposing building whose great ballroom and central 'Palm Court' had been divided into small offices by wooden partitions. I was in the basement, behind bars, working for SOE as a cypher clerk. Subtraction without 'carrying over' seemed wonderfully simple, but it was some weeks before I could memorise anything more than the figures for 'and'; other more experienced girls worked like lightening, chattering as they did so about the dresses they were going to wear for their evenings' 'date'. At first I was interested in the subject of the telegrams, until so many of them complained of the restraining activities of the other organisation MI 5 . . . 'we propose' . . . some exciting adventure in a fishing boat . . . 'but so-and-so does not agree . . .'. Finally the ship carrying Legation staff from Bucharest arrived at the quayside. Denis was to proceed in the few weeks' time to Trebizond. In the main courtyard of the Consulate in Istanbul, crates of the personal effects of Sir Reginald Hoare, ex-Minister in Bucharest, were stacked to await shipment and Lady Hoare, an eccentric character, was unpacking a few of them as Denis and I passed by. She had treated him coldly in Bucharest, saying that he had opened a window in the Chancery, in which she was camping after an earthquake had made the upper storey of the building unsafe, and had given her a cold. But now she relented. 'If you are going to Trebizond,' she said, 'you will need a steam kettle; it will be cold in the winter. And here are some deck quoits too, for exercise.' She added a dozen small lampshades for chandeliers, and presented them all to us warmly.

In the end I did not go home, as Denis sent for me to join him. Life in Trezibond was very restricted, and he could not get a maid to work for him as a man alone. He stayed at first in the Yesil Yurt Hotel, made famous by Rose Macaulay in her Towers of Trebizond.

Chapter Four

Trebizond, 1941

A letter home:–

"I have never seen a place with so many children, they are all over the streets and greens, nearly all bare-footed and in long cotton frocks like nightdresses, nearly to their feet, the little boys in long striped trousers too. The older ones wear clogs, just flat wooden soles with a strap over the instep, which make a lovely hollow sound, quite musical, as they go over the stony streets and paths.

We live in the Consulate which is a white, two-storeyed house up in the higher part of the town, facing out over the sea and towards the mountains of the Lower Caucasus. The garden is in terraces, the top one of stone with a vine covering one end of it under which we can sit in summer. On the lower ones are fruit trees and a cypress, a landmark which we can see from far off when we go for walks. In a small room by the entrance gate sit the two 'kavasses' who guard us and bring in visitors, and in a low wing of the house, at the side of the garden and once the 'Harem' or women's quarters, is the kitchen, presided over by Eminé, one of the few women we can get to serve in a foreign household, and who will appear before men, even though veiled.

I have just recovered from a fever, lasting three days, a kind of malaria which is apparently common here; Eminé looked after me and we decided not to get a doctor. Her cure was to tie sliced raw potatoes with salt round my head, which was very cool, and lasted longer than a wet handkerchief. Then she massaged me with powdered quinine and lemon, and after this tied me up in a blanket and eiderdown until I perspired. She also made chicken and meat soups for me, and it seems to be quite satisfactory.

Since we have been here there have been various difficulties over food, most of it having to come by ship through the Black Sea and taking much longer than usual owing to the danger of mines. Very often when there is a delay the ships' crew and passengers have to start eating the flour, salt, etc. intended for all the small villages along the coast. At the moment we have, in the Consulate, no sugar at all. There has been none available in the town for a month, and yesterday the small stock that we had ran out. For our tea it does not matter as we do not take it, but for coffee and for cooking in general it is very difficult, also for cocoa and other hot drinks now that the weather is colder. The sweet shops are practically empty, as everyone is buying anything sweet that they can find, and I am just going to buy some chocolate that is left, in order to make a drink of it with milk. The Turks all take two or three or five, or even up to eight or nine lumps in their tea in extreme cases, so that when they come as guests one does not know what to give them; however some local substitutes such as raisins will do, and the cafés now serve these in tea. No one we know has enough sugar to lend, and with the Turks, either we do not like to ask them or if we do, they say anyhow that they haven't any because they are afraid of being hung, which is the penalty for hoarding. Besides raisins, though, one can still find a few biscuits in the town made from powdered nuts, which have an effect of sweetness. There is a shortage of flour also, and complications over bread. For a week we had heavy, sodden maize bread, because though a lot of flour had arrived in town it was sold free and in a moment was all bought up, as people bake their own bread usually. The government now sell the better bread which is being

The British Consulate, Trebizond

View from the Consulate

made in small quantities, to officials at a lower price than to private people, and as these officials are the same people, in many cases, who snapped up the flour, they now have good bread *and* flour, while everyone else has none.

Storms on the Black Sea also make the ships late, and erratic. There are storms every year on the same day, or hardly more than a day out, and they are marked on the calendar, called the Storm of the Chestnuts, or of The Grape Harvest, or the Frogs, and so on. This week unfortunately there are two, with only a day between.

The dresses I wrote for from England have just arrived, taking four months! I wonder what the fashion is now in France and in England, and what is the length of dresses. In Istanbul girls still do their hair on top of their head in curls, as before the war in England. One has to do one's own hair here, none of the women would go to a barbers shop. One cannot buy shampoo, and I make my own with melted soap in hot water. All nice soap, French and English, and of course all cosmetics, are practically finished. The Turks make their own but they do not seem nice, rather like Woolworths quality. Cotton thread is also nearly run out, as they always imported Coates and the French D.M.C. before. Another thing you cannot get at all is a torch battery, if there was a black-out we would have to use an oil lantern to get about with.

It is odd how we live with 'primitive' things quite naturally now. As there is plenty of time for everything it is no trouble to light a geyser with wood, as we do to make a bath, and to heat all the rooms with wood in black, workshop type stoves with pipes running across the ceiling, and cooking on a wood stove (though quite a modern shape and with a good oven), or with the shells of hazel nuts which are produced here, and which make a fire keep in for ages. Old Eminé manages with nothing in the way of dusters, mops etc., but only rags, and for washing dishes she ties a few cock feathers together, and sweeps with a bunch of dried grasses. She cleans the silver and the pots and pans, which are copper lined with tin, with handfuls of wood ash from the stove. She also suggests preserving eggs for the winter by laying them in ashes. Of course in England it is really simpler to use modern things because you could not easily get wood for your stove or grass brooms, etc . . .

Eminé invited me to have food at her family's cottage in a village up above Trebizond last Sunday. It was a hot day with a view of snow mountains in the distance towards Russia, and of all the coastline in between with its little bays and wooded inlets with villages. Fabri, the Maltese secretary at the Consulate, came with me, as he has known Eminé for years, and we had a little table set for us under a tree in the chicken yard, with children running about, barefoot of course, and with gypsy earrings. One of them was quite blond; many people here have Russian blood. No one could eat with us as it is Ramadan, but they killed a chicken, made a 'pilaff' with it, and baked potatoes, and coffee, as we sat there. The other women, who do not appear before men without something over their heads (with us, though not with strangers, or with Turks who visit us, Eminé often lets her headscarf fall back on her shoulders) peeped from windows at us, but on the whole they did not seem curious.

Eminé recounted her grievances against the kavasses, Hussein and Osman. She says they take commission on all the things they buy us, that their chatter in the streets with everyone. She herself is much more capable than either of them, and she treats them like small boys, at least the younger, who is forty-six. Very often she swears at them, and then *they* complain to us. The son of Osman often takes his place when he is ill with bronchitis, but he is so lazy and does no other work at all, because Osman is so well paid (he gets almost as much as a Turkish bank director here) that he does not need to.

We have altered the rooms for the coming winter, and now live in the two front ones which get the most sun, and have shut up the others. Our furniture is gradually increasing by little things; I hope we shall be able to get some of it

Denis and Iona Wright, Trebizond 1941

home. The Irish linen sheets are much admired and one of the pillow cases was stolen; however I have everything else and the hand-towels especially are very nice. The maids here, of course, do all the washing, and Eminé also washes Denis' suits, even his raincoat, because there are no cleaners shops. I do all my own things actually, because they spoil silk by rubbing it. One American we once met, who lived on the Black Sea, said he gave a suit to his man-servant to take to the cleaners, and later he saw it being scrubbed in sea water down in the bay.

At the moment, because this is a good place for silks, I buy lengths to make up into dresses later, and use them now for table-cloths, cushions, curtains, etc. because there is no good dress-maker here. In the next place we go to, no one will know that they were curtains. Silk is cheap and cotton is expensive, sewing silk costs practically nothing and a reel of Coates cotton is charged at about five times as much. There are still good silk stockings, I get mine for the equivalent of 12/6 a pair, but they do not have very hard wear here. The price goes up by about sixpence a month. There are also insects which eat them, and if you keep them on too long, they will rot.

There is not much shortage of other things yet, besides food. The worst is of rubber, there is hardly any at all and almost all private cars are off the road, and a lot of buses stopped. Tyres for lorries now cost a hundred pounds each, and the roads being so rough they do not last long. The price of a taxi to go to Erzerum, the nearest railway stop 125 miles away, is now twenty pounds. The bus is still cheap but uncomfortable, and takes fourteen hours, a bit ignominious for the British Consul, and the German Consul goes by taxi!

There is always a quantity of rose-pink face powder in the shops, because being near the Persian border the Turks do not want to look like Persians or Arabs, and if they happen to have dark skins they disguise it. I had to get some from Istanbul, by way of the old French Consul here, who is retired, but cannot get back to France. He is about sixty, quite a dandy with a small pointed beard, buttoned boots and high stiff collars. He is quite an encyclopedia and can talk about all sorts of unusual things. He seems to know all about face-powder, although he is a bachelor, so I asked him to choose some for me when he went on holiday to Istanbul, and a careful selection of very subtle shades was the result.

The transit trade between Germany and Persia is now stopped by our intervention there; and there is less work for Denis to do, recording it. Our idea now is to see more of the countryside, as well as to continue learning Turkish; the former will cause much interest. The Turks here are friendly, but they live so differently from us that we do not get beyond a certain point with them. I would like to have some European women to go out with, and have a chat over coffee somewhere. I don't know what would happen if two women went into one of the coffee shops. Nothing of course, but I couldn't get any woman here to do it. The other foreign couples will not take part in anything Turkish, but are always scornful and superior about them. The result is that one has a series of tea-parties with these non-Turks, about three a week, and about three times a week some of them visit us, but it is rather ridiculous having nothing to do all day long, and then having to dress up and parade out as if at last you were going to relax, and give yourself up to recreation and enjoyment, when there is still nothing to do or to talk about. I do housework in the mornings, but in a very general sense, picking and arranging flowers, sewing, framing pictures, making small bits of furniture, etc. In the afternoons we usually go for a walk, either into the country or round the old ruins of Trebizond, where you can, bit by bit, see the old form of the town as a fortress, though there are houses built in and out of it now. Then there may be a tea-party somewhere, or perhaps we call on a Turkish family after office hours and have coffee and a sweet liqueur with them. One day we met the Chief of the

Military Police, very grand, polite and formal. We were honoured by his asking us to have a glass of tea in the public gardens. As we were sitting there he looked down at my shoes and said "How much did they cost?"

There is one Turkish family, not Trebizond people, who are very hospitable and usually make us stay on to a meal with them, which the foreign colony never do, they always ask you for a definite time and no more, not that they are not quite kind but they live in a dull routine which it would never enter their heads to break, whereas one really has endless time and so have they. But on the whole the Turks like you to announce a visit the day before. I find that the women are not naturally very tidy; they loll about gossiping in curling pins and old shoes on most days. They hardly ever see their husbands, who eat out with other men, so they have no need to dress for anybody. They welcome the chance to dress up. If you go unexpectedly they spend the whole time apologising for one thing or another, their own slippers, the fact that one of the carpets is outside being beaten, and that they have not a cake ready for you. Otherwise their conversation is about illnesses, whether you intend to have any children or not, how much your clothes cost, how you curl your hair etc. Once we had a family to dinner, a couple with two children. They discussed every dish, the children upset things and climbed up and down off their chairs, the mother pushed the hat she was wearing on to the back of her head and left it perched there, and about half way through, while waiting in between courses, she picked up the plates and examined the markings on the back. Eminé took a dislike to them because they were rather dark-skinned and she said they were Persians.

An Englishman called here yesterday, off the boat for Istanbul, on his way to Africa. He has been working in some copper mines near here for two years, in a small village which is completely isolated by snow in winter, and with only two other Englishmen for company. One of them also came to see us, a Cornishman, who had only seen London for the first time on his way out here. He had once played in a Salvation Army Band in Redruth, but had been turned out for looking over a wall at a Circus. He seems to get on well with the Turks, speaks a little Turkish and likes their food.

Old Eminé had a heart attack a short time ago, but has recovered. She thought she was going to die, and a stream of relations came to visit her; in the kitchen there was a row of shoes, which they take off when going into a house. She seems to have plenty of energy again now, as long as I don't ask her to do some unpleasant job. She still shouts at the two kavasses, and they get furious with her, but when she was ill they were very concerned. She goes about in a pair of wooden sandals and Denis' old socks, and a bundle of clothes. She dyes her hair bright orange with henna, as the peasants all do when they go grey, saying it is good for the eyesight. She looked extra-ordinary when she was ill, sitting cross-legged on her bed, without her usual headdress and only a piece of white cotton bound round her orange hair which was in wispy pigtails. She has a very pleasant old face, and a good sense of humour, and tells people that she is very fond of us. She brings us milk from her cow which is called 'Binbasha' (Colonel). It is odd to think how much she has not seen, a train for instance; she has never left Trebizond except once for Ordu, not far down the coast, where she was driven by the Russians in the Great War. Her husband was killed in one of the Balkan wars, and four of her children died.

We went recently to the cinema (where on our first visit a rat ran along the balustrade of our box) with a Persian couple, the secretary of the Persian Consulate and his wife. She is much more talkative than the Turkish women, and her husband speaks French while she knows a little English. He had a great idea of his position when they married and told her he would be Consul-General in London, and she was eager to see Paris as she loves clothes and had also heard that Arab girls had a great success in Europe. Then they came by bus to Trebizond and have been here ever since; she has not even been to Istanbul. He told Denis that he was offered Cairo as a post, but that he had to refuse it because his wife was too fond of an Egyptian film star she has seen here in the cinema. Denis puts up with him and his almost un-intelligible French because they are both amusing and friendly. When we go to any public function they sit with us as colleagues and he has on his visiting card 'Premier Secrétaire du Consulat d'Iran', a post which does not exist. She is very colourful, with dusky skin and gay make-up, small coloured combs in her hair and dangling turquoise earrings; in an old Persian shawl at a dance she looked richer than anyone there.

Eminé always asks about the war, though she does not know much about this one. When I say that it is terribly cold now in Russia, she begins to cry, rocking herself from side to side and talking to Allah about the poor Russian soldiers; and when I mention the Germans, being so far from home fighting the Russians, she cries for them.

Today is sunny and clear: a view of the whole of the snowy mountains behind Rize and the sea very blue. It makes one feel energetic. The best thing is to go down into the town and through the shops and open market; in the afternoon it becomes too cold and then too dark for shopping. Yesterday we walked up one of the valleys behind Trebizond, finding the road roughly paved in the same way as the ancient transit road to Persia is, in another valley, also bridges well-made, and wide, as if it was once important. The valley is narrow, but there was the sun shining straight down it, very good weather for a walk in spite of the mud where the paving stones had sunk or been taken away to build a house. There were practically no houses, though, and we met only half a dozen people in an hour, two women with huge burdens of fire-wood and maize stalks, bare-footed; two boys chopping wood by a stream; and two men with a laden donkey.

In mid-January, 1942, we were called to Ankara, and travelled by ship to Samsun on the Black Sea coast, where we took the train for a journey lasting thirty-six hours, delayed by the snow, and with no sleeper or restaurant-car; we fed on some cold birds shot by our Consul in Samsun. No-one met us in Ankara and all hotels were full, so eventually we called on an Embassy secretary at 4 a.m., and were kindly given a room in his house.

We stayed for four months, Denis working for the Commercial Secretary at the Embassy, while I worked for the Press Attaché. We had been homesick in Trebizond, and as Denis said, it was "nice to see grey flannels and smart women again". We took a flat in the Yeni Şehir district, and a part-time maid, and enjoyed the social life of ski-ing on Sundays and parties for the rest of the week. Ankara, like Istanbul, was full of the intrigue of any war-time neutral capital, but of some gaiety too, to the tunes of 'J'attendrai' and 'Lili Marlene'. The main centre was the Palace Hotel, and the restaurant 'Carpiç' where British and Germans would sit at separate tables. The German Ambassador, Herr von Papen, was slightly wounded, and his assailant blown to pieces, in front of our car as I drove to work one morning. We encountered the famous 'Cicero', serving drinks at the British Embassy.

But Denis became impatient after a time to return to Trebizond. I went off to Jerusalem to stay with the Kendalls and buy some English toothpaste and some ready-made clothes, while Denis also took a fortnight's holiday in Palestine. From there he did go back, by boat, and I joined him. He made several trips by horse, horse and cart, and lorry into the interior, and in the intervals became tennis champion of Trebizond! We had some English visitors, which broke the monotony, and during the fighting on the Black Sea a German bomber made a forced landing behind the town, and a Russian dinghy arrived with survivors from Sevastopol, asking for our help with food and petrol to get them to Batum.

With the Russian victory at Stalingrad, and the change in our favour in North Africa, Denis began to feel that he must get back to the centre of things. In December I returned to Istanbul and took a job in the Press Office of the Embassy.

Ted Peck (now Sir Edward and our oldest F.O. friend), armed with whisky and cigarettes, was sent from Ankara to spend a lonely Christmas with Denis who told him that he would resign rather than spend any longer in Trebizond. After being summoned to Ankara "for consultation" Denis was eventually, in April 1943, sent to take charge of the busy consulate in Mersin on the Mediterranean.

Chapter Five

Trebizond, 1942

I don't mind being back in Trabzon. There is not much more to do, but the difficult things that were new last year are not so evident now. There are still no women who play tennis, but I go and watch every day or so to get them used to seeing a woman there. They now ask me if I can play, as they see women playing on the films, and there is a film now about Ankara and the tennis club there, so I shall soon knock-up with Denis I expect, and it may develop. We have been one long walk, up to a peak behind Trabzon which is said to have had a Greek statue on it, in 'olden times', and we are going a longer walk and climb to an abandoned Greek monastery, perched up in the rocks, which has interesting frescoes in it.

We have had the Consulate distempered and painted. I thought of a lemon yellow but it came out a pale cream which is not bad, they haven't the finer shades in the shops. I got some bright red and yellow lengths of cotton, which are really made for belts for the peasants, they wind them round several times over white breeches, but they make nice curtains. Then I got a stone water jar and painted it cream too, I meant to paint a green squiggle round it, but unfortunately it is a bit porous and no good for flowers as it leaves a damp stain on tables. It looks pretty with a bunch of roses, pink and white and yellow with a strong scent.

There is a lovely smell of orange blossom in Near Eastern gardens in the spring, and after that of honeysuckle and roses. In Adana, in the south east of Turkey, where it is hotter and people sleep on the roofs (I saw on my way to Palestine) there are gardens with pools in the middle, lots of orange trees, and turtle doves cooing, it is quite like Arabian nights stories, and although the gardens were weedy really, and they have no idea of complicated gardening, they were such sleepy cool places you could imagine people just sitting and sitting in them and feeling quite remote, almost melting into them, in the shade which the sound of the water makes cooler.

Our Eminé is going to her village, a few miles away, for a month or so's rest in the hot weather, and we are having a boy instead, who worked for some Americans for several years. We are just beginning a series of tea-parties, as with the foreign colony who keep French manners it is the new-comers who call first and we have done that, but it is now difficult to return hospitality without flour, there is none at all except some very rough brown stuff for bread, so we have to make cakes of powdered hazel-nuts or walnuts.

Chapter Six

The Ambassador and the Cream Jug

In the summer of 1943 we returned to Trebizond from Mersin to open up the Consulate for the visit of our Ambassador from Ankara, his wife, secretary* and chauffeur. As the Consulate had been empty for some time, we had to collect all we could to make it habitable. Unfortunately the Turkish President was also expected to arrive, and the Hotel had sent all its plate and cutlery up to the small village where he was to have a welcoming party before reaching Trebizond in the evening. So we borrowed from the foreign colony as well. We had always lived there perfectly well with very few knives and forks and plates, but for visitors there were things like 'morning tea', and finger bowls. Milk jugs are difficult to obtain in Turkey as they take lemon in their tea. We also had only one very small tin tray and one rather large one made of tiles with pictures of flowers on it. I worried a great deal over the jugs, and asked the kavasses to find one, but it was impossible until seven o'clock in the morning as all our neighbours were keeping Ramadan and we could not disturb them the night before, when they were sleeping after the day's fasting. Hussein, the younger kavass, at last arrived with a large three pint jug, the sort one would find in a dairy.

*Ted Peck.

67

So the Ambassador's wife had a tiny tray which would not even hold the tea-pot as well as the milk and the sugar, and the Ambassador had the huge jug and huge tray. The next day Lady Hugessen told me not to trouble to give her any, so perhaps she had seen the difficulty. She was shy and did not talk much and I wondered what she thought of our home-made curtains from Turkish material meant for head scarves, still hanging in the windows. In the evening when Denis was entertaining the Ambassador at a dinner for men only in the hotel, and had taken Hussein with him, old Osman served us at dinner, but as he suffered from asthma he was too exhausted by the walk from the kitchen to serve us, but just planted the dishes down on the table between us. At the Hotel the dinner was very successful. The Turks liked the whisky which the Ambassador had brought, and the cocktail which Denis mixed beforehand (gin, Egyptian vermouth and a Turkish orange liqueur).

The next day there was a lunch with the Governor. Lunches are still in the old style, everyone eating out of the same large bowl, and all the food in different order from ours. The guests were very much the same as the night before, except for a few more officials, among them the Persian Consul, a good friend of ours, but very elaborate in manner. He bowed low over the Ambassador's hand, and made a long speech in French, which the Ambassador had to cut short as he saw that the Turks did not want a Persian to occupy so much of his time. There followed a speech from the Director of the Agricultural Bank, also in French, but he had been drinking both whisky and wine and referred to the Ambassador as a 'champignon' instead of a 'Champion'.

The visit seemed to have been a success, at least from the Turkish point of view, but I was relieved when it was all over. Trebizond looked lovely to us in the warm autumn weather, with sun all day and the sea dead calm. The Consulate is simple and pretty and cosy, the sun pours in in the morning for breakfast, the kavasses and the woman servant are loyal and tactful, always there but not obtrusive. The garden and flowers, bright geraniums along the terrace; and the cat which we had left last year was still sitting there cleaning herself or chasing lizards; she had three kittens now in the chicken run and was very content.

We ourselves had come by train and car from Ankara, taking twelve hours along the transit road from Erzerum to Trebizond, and we were supposed to go back the same way, following the Ambassador's car. We started off in our hired car an hour before them, but they soon overtook us. At ten o'clock we stuck, going over the first pass, and had to spend the night there, going back to Trebizond the next day to take the ship.

At the Inn on the top of the pass we found a well-known Trebizond figure known as "Kaptan Bey", who spends the summer months there in a tent. He belongs to the Nemlizade family, and since the death of his wife some years ago, in a motor accident not far from the pass, he brings two of his daughters up with him to cook, but is very strict with them and does not allow them to see any men. If they marry it will be by arrangement, though they have rich relations in Istanbul and when their mother was alive used to go there every year. The old man is an impressive figure, in a huge black tweed suit with knickerbockers, a white flannel shirt and a black tam-o-shanter, he looked like Henry the Eighth standing, feet apart, at the door of the Inn to welcome visitors. He knows everyone who goes along the transit road. Only the President he is not much interested in, and he regards the gendarme post at the top of the pass, where a show is made of looking at papers, as quite superfluous and stupid. He is scornful of the young gendarmes' patriotism for the new Turkey. He is intelligent but eccentric, and has never worked, so that his children are not well off and his sons, at least, resent it. He travelled once in Europe, but speaks no French.

We had a long conversation with him over supper, difficult for us being entirely in Turkish; but it was a good meal and afterwards he gave us his room with a clean bed and leather covers bought years ago in England, while he himself slept in his tent, where he keeps his shooting kit. It was very cold at night but sunny and clear in the morning. The pass is between grassy hills, with a wide view of the mountain-tops all round and of the transit road winding steeply for miles. We were up at six o'clock and sat outside reading, while Kaptan Bey shaved himself at the fountain, then Denis was invited by one of the gendarmes to have tea with them, and I went to the daughters' room upstairs to talk to them.

Suddenly, and while Kaptan Bey was still at the fountain, the delegation to meet the President arrived, including the governor and five or six carloads of retainers who had started at 3 a.m. from Trebizond. Kaptan Bey received them graciously, in his shirt sleeves and with a towel piled on top of his head, razor in hand. He has a wide, military moustache which looks fierce, but a gentle smile. After the governor had rather reluctantly stopped to greet him, one or two of his special friends dropped behind and we had tea together. I remembered the cream jugs in the Consulate, and my worry over them. But here was Kaptan Bey, who would have received the President himself, when he passed this way, with the same charming informality.

Outside the British Consulate, Mersin 1943

Chapter Seven

Mersin, 1943

The little church of St. Sophia, fading into the mist, was our last sight of Trebizond from the sea. It stood on a grassy platform above the coast road, surrounded by the red-tiled roofs of peasant cottages, each with their plot of maize and tobacco. During the war it was used as a munitions dump, and we could only look at it from the outside, admiring its three porches with marble pillars and intricate stone carving.

Of the same period, though on a site regarded as holy from much earlier times, was the monastery of Sumelas, or Maryam Ana, thirty miles inland, on the way to Persia. William Palgrave, when Consul in Trebizond, reaching it by horse in the 1860's, describes the impressive setting which it still has today... "after rounding the foot of a monstrous rock, we see the white walls of the convent, suspended like a birds' nest in the air, far overhead ..."

Denis made three trips to this site, and I made one, by hired car and then on foot to the base of the rocky mountainside, from where we climbed the twisting, steep path through a pine forest, dotted with flowering azaleas and rhododendrons in spring. Palgrave was received hospitably by the monks, and given food and a bed for the night, but when we reached it we found an empty shell behind the four tiers of windows visible from the valley below. The chapel, in a cave round which the whole building had been constructed had the remains of frescoes, but had been ransacked by the Turks after the forced

71

departure of the Greeks in 1923. After Denis had made three visits there the Turks began to wonder what his interest in it was, and put it 'out of bounds'. Most of our movements were watched and it was difficult for them to understand the fascination of such a place, especially as it was a long journey from the main road.

Palgrave also described the climate of Trebizond, which together with the scenery reminded him of North Wales. In autumn the sea mists were so thick below our house that we could not see the ships in the harbour, or even the sheep which grazed on the piece of waste land over the garden wall; we could only hear the muffled sound of their bells as they moved.

The new post to which Denis was appointed in April 1943 was Mersin in southern Turkey. Instead of the soft green hills and forested mountains of the north we were in a flat seaport, some miles from the Taurus mountains, with a hot and humid climate for most of the year, the rich farm land behind it producing oranges, olives and grapes.

The consulate building was in the centre of the town, standing in a small garden. Several tall palm trees shaded the roof on which we had our breakfast in the cool of the early morning, and from which we could see camels bringing fruit and vegetables to a market outside our walls. The consular office, dining-room and kitchen were on the ground floor, together with a large central hall which, unlike Trebizond, was often filled with people. There was much business connected with the port, and with a company of Royal Engineers who were camped outside the town, in the guise of contractors, building roads. In addition there were a number of British, some with wives, employed in the Consulate and the government owned United Kingdom Commercial Corporation.

We lived on the upper floor of the building, and were waited on by a Maltese maid called Antoinette, and her Greek husband, Leonidas. Leonidas was an excellent and conscientious cook, but his wife found life difficult with a small baby, living in one room above the kitchen, having come herself from Istanbul. The heat in summer was stifling. We would take several showers during the night to keep cool, and wait for the slight breeze which would come from the mountains in the early morning and enable us to sleep for a few hours. From our roof we could see the iron bedsteads and rolls of bedding of our neighbours who slept on their roofs as did all the poorer people in these southern towns. I wrote home:–

July 1943

"Here it is very hot now . . . So far, every Sunday we have been along the coast to bathe, it is perfect now to drop into the water out of the heat and sprawl about, it is just not too shallow and not too deep, and there are rocks or there is sand, whichever you want. We take tea with us usually, cucumber and tomatoes and hard-boiled eggs (two each!) and three or four thermos' of tea. I don't make jam sandwiches because sugar is so expensive that jam is a luxury, though there is all the fruit you want to make it with here, I have lately been trying to make lemon curd, but took a long time because I didn't realise that Mrs Beaton calls it Lemon Cheese.

Will you send me the recipe for chocolate fudge? Though I suppose you have not made it for some time. It would be very useful for me to give to callers in the afternoons. Turks usually give coffee and sweets of some sort. We have no coffee for the moment, things like that simply vanish here. Can you get rice in England? I suppose not. We have it quite often. Pilaff is the Turkish dish I like best! We have it with curry, too, as the last consul left us a tin. We have five hens now, and they lay a few eggs. I hope to get a cock and have chicks next year. Sugar now costs the equivalent of nine-and-six a pound!

Do you still do the school canteen? I can't *imagine* how you do a meal for fourpence. And is fourpence really all the children can afford? Our lunches here cost about three shillings per head."

Denis was busy all day with questions concerning the port,

the Engineers' camp, or with Turkish officials, far more accessible than in Trebizond. He particularly liked the Governor, or *Vali* of Mersin, called Tefik Gür, who was energetic, practical and helpful. There was little time for our walks of exploration. Denis would sometimes get up early and go down to a beach on a bicycle to have a swim, but in the afternoons we were either taking a 'siesta' or preparing to call on someone, or to receive callers. Our predecessor had made friends almost exclusively among the large Syrian community who, though Turkish citizens, were Christians, retaining contacts with members of their families in Syria and Lebanon. They were rich and were not popular with the Turks. In the local business men's club there was a notice 'Turkish only to be spoken', referring to the Syrians' habit of talking French and Arabic among themselves. When we had established some friendships with the Turks, we began to accept invitations to the gay parties given by the Syrians in their lavishly furnished homes, where there would be wine to drink, and dancing, and where the daughters of the house would ask their friends among the Royal Engineers.

But at every weekend we would go out into the country, in a borrowed jeep, as we had no car, and with friends from the Engineers' camp who wanted to get away for a time from their communal living. We drove along the coast on a dusty road, and picnicked and swam in one of the small sandy bays, completely deserted and ideal for bathing. Behind us the ground was broken by boulders of rock and red earth, with oleanders, olives and fig trees growing wild amongst them and here and there, half hidden, were the remains of another civilisation, not Greek but Roman . . . tombs, fallen temples, baths, reservoirs, aquaducts. These dotted the coastline as far as we could go on a day's journey, and we would scramble among them, only meeting an occasional goat or goatsherd. Some columns still standing on the beach indicated the Roman harbour of Pompeopolis, and some way inland on a hillside was the beautiful temple at Olba, where a peasant remarked . . . "how well those people built . . ."

The Turks of Mersin showed no interest in these sites, and as it was wartime, no one else visited them either. Almost by chance we found the enormous chasm in the ground which was the Corycean oracle described by the Roman historian Strabo, but not re-discovered until 1852. It was far larger than a tennis court, with sheer sides and a church in a cave at the bottom, where the rushing sound of water underground gave the place its reputation for supernatural power. Nearby was a smaller chasm, equally deep and forbidding, and the two were known by the Turks as *Gennet* and *Gehenneh*, or 'Heaven' and 'Hell'. We were never tired of looking at these wonders, and took any visitors we might have to see them.

The *Vali*, on the other hand, was only interested in modernising the town. It was not an old settlement and had few interesting features. A row of eucalyptus trees along the sea front gave shade in summer and were graceful, pink and grey leafed trees. He thought them ugly and cut them all down, replacing them by square flower beds filled with geraniums.

One of his ideas was to build a club for businessmen, larger than the present one and to be paid for by a tax on local merchants. He consulted Denis as he said the English were famous for their clubs. One of the Royal Engineers who was an architect was asked to produce a design, and this was used later, but not until after we had left; and when finished the building fell down, not because the design was at fault but because of bad workmanship. But a building which was successfully constructed to the Vali's wishes was the *halkevi* or 'People's House', a centre for lectures and classes in higher education, to which Denis was able to persuade him to add classes in Turkish for foreigners.

We frequently met him on social occasions, which he attended with his daughter, an intelligent and studious girl who wanted to become a school-mistress and was learning English, which she already knew well enough to translate for us. We were invited with them one day to a circumcision party given by a local rich family. Rich Turks who had sons who had reached the age of six or seven would invite poorer people's sons to join them in this ceremony, and this time the whole house was open for celebration. Passing from room to room we came on seven small boys in a large double bed, covered with a silk embroidered quilt, and wearing coloured paper hats on their dark hair, their eyes slightly glazed from the drugs they had been given, and attended by an old woman who sat at the foot of the bed. The Vali's daughter cheerfully translated for us the importance of the ceremony, and we all enjoyed a buffet supper with Turkish wine, and coffee. Coffee was a luxury, and sugar by now cost the equivalent of seven-and-sixpence a pound.

It was the habit of the Turks to drink coffee four or five times a morning and afternoon in their offices, as well as at home, and to offer it to all callers. Small boys brought it from the nearest coffee-house on a brass tray suspended on three chains from a ring which they balanced skilfully as they ran along the streets and up stairs.

Because of the shortage the Vali decreed that coffee-drinking in the offices should cease, for the reason too that he thought it was a lazy habit. The coffee, made with an equal proportion of sugar, was strong and sweet, and was as much a habit as the smoking of the *narghileh* or 'hubble-bubble'.

Before I left, the Vali and his daughter were at a dinner in his house, in honour of a British ship which was in port, at which Denis remarked on the particularly delicious sweet, a kind of 'rhum baba'. The daughter, dutifully translating, repeated the Turkish name as her father reminded her of it; "Kadin Gobeye, it is called", she said, "Kadin Gobeye . . . this is . . . lady's navel". "Yes," said the Vali in a gay mood, and raising his glass, "Let us all drink . . . to ladies' navels!"

At the end of 1943, after Italy surrendered, and the Mediterranean was open to shipping again, I flew down to Cairo in an American Air Force 'plane with women and children from our Embassy in Ankara and the British chaplain and his family from Istanbul.

After staying a short time with the Kendalls – Mila Kendall was broadcasting news to Bulgaria – we were put on board a ship in convoy from East Africa – civil servants from the Sudan, Kenya and Uganda, together with missionaries, one of whom shared my cabin – for a journey to Glasgow which took six weeks and included an encounter with a German bomber from Crete which sunk one ship, though the crew and passengers survived and were taken aboard other ships.

Denis followed just over a year later, in January, 1945. Meanwhile, I was conscripted as a hospital cleaner but managed to join one sister and a brother-in-law in the Ministry of Information, where I was a filing clerk in the Censorship Department; one of the censors was the mother of a soldier at Arnhem and I remember the tension of those days. I lived at home again in Sussex, when flying bombs rattled over our trains to London.

When Denis got home he worked in the Consular department of the Foreign office, and then joined the Ottoman Bank, but he did not care for banking in London, and rejoined the Foreign Office. Our first post abroad was to be Belgrade.

Chapter Eight

The People's Republic, 1946–8

In September 1946, I passed through Trieste on my way to Belgrade, where Denis had been made Commercial Secretary at the British Embassy. Trieste was full of British soldiers and the hotel where I stayed was reserved for British officers, their wives, children and nannies; it was on the water-front where a ship of the American navy was moored, with a dance going on on board. All the women seemed to be wearing smart Italian clothes and to have the latest hair-style, so I went to a hairdresser while waiting to continue my journey by road, the rail between Trieste and Ljublana having been badly damaged in the war and not yet repaired. I eventually left in a jeep driven by an official of UNRRA and joined the train again with the help of the British consul in Ljublana, continuing my way slowly with crowds of other passengers, for another twenty-four hours. Breakfast on the train consisted of black bread and olives with a little tea, or a bottle of the national drink, 'Slivovitz'. We had to go carefully over many bridges which were being repaired, and the corridors being so full of people, the only way to go from one's carriage to the restaurant car was to run along the platform when we stopped in a station. I was taking much of our luggage with me, several large trunks, as Denis had flown from Bari in Italy and could take little.

He was already installed in the house of his predecessor, a 'villa' in what had once been a smart suburb of Belgrade, called Senjak, with tree-lined, cobbled streets and gardens filled with fruit trees and flowers. It had belonged to a diplomat of the pre-war regime, who now lived quietly with his wife on the Adriatic coast, where some small property remained to him. His father had been a famous artist and his pictures decorated our walls, together with smaller ornaments which he collected from time to time to sell in order to buy food and medicine for which he was allowed no ration cards.

A wide oak staircase led from the hall to the bedrooms above, and once again we could breakfast on a balcony, this time overlooking the river Sava, on whose junction with the Danube Belgrade was built, and across it to a wide plain stretching, if one could have seen so far, to Hungary.

Together with the house we had a maid called Slavka, a ruddy-faced, plump and sturdy girl who cooked, cleaned, washed and shopped for us. She kept hens in the back garden which supplied us with eggs, and she had a kitten which followed her everywhere. We were amused at first by her cheerful chatter, but soon found her too inquisitive about any guests who came to the house. Denis would deliberately mislead her by saying that they were Russians. She told me that the tinned food supplied by UNRRA was poisoned and refused to eat it. Eventually, as our entertaining increased, and friends would visit us from England, we employed a second servant, Magda, who was a friend of Slavka, but was a sad, serious girl, whose husband was in one of the largest prisons, for what reason we never found out; she took food to him every fortnight and Slavka did not, in front of her, show too much enthusiasm for the present government. Magda worked hard and seldom spoke; she looked tired and nervous and we never learnt anything of her background; only occasionally she would smile and she never seemed to expect gratitude for anything.

In Belgrade we Westerners lived entirely amongst ourselves, and there were very few of us outside the 'diplomatic' circle; only a handful of journalists, and businessmen seeking compensation for their property which had been confiscated lived in the Majestic Hotel and entertained each other to drinks in the bar there. The British Council and other cultural organisations were closely linked with their respective Embassies, though they could have some contact with the translators and secretaries whom the Jugoslavs allowed them to employ. These would go to the houses of foreigners very rarely, and never invite them to theirs. The Jugoslavs would go to receptions in the Embassies, but never to private houses, and for the two-and-a-half years that we were there we only once had the young son of an ex-minister to see us, in great secrecy, and once visited his parents where they sat with all windows closed and shutters down, almost too nervous to speak about plans to escape. The Communist authorities discouraged all contacts with westerners. When occasionally our Ambassador managed to entertain a Yugoslav Minister or official we regarded these tie-less ex-Partisans with great curiosity, while the old Embassy butler complained that they stubbed out their cigarettes on the polished tables. Many were greatly admired by the British

Iona with Peter Wright, Assistant Military Attaché of the British Embassy, and Denis on left with the American Consul's wife, Belgrade 1946

81

who had fought with them in Tito's campaigns, but in the first years of peace all normal, casual contacts between friends had to be denied.

I had a teacher, Vera Popovic, who came to our house every week for two hours, and who told me about the shops where I could find things not in the big government store, about her ski-ing in winter, and the theatres and concerts which she enjoyed. But none of this could be shared, we could never join her ski-ing, though we might meet her on the slopes, and if we met in the theatre we could only nod. Slavka, Magda, and later Maritza who took Slavka's place, were the only Jugoslavs we knew well. It was like watching a play, and for us a sombre one, but to them, after the war, it was something better. There were food shortages and for us there was a 'Diplomatic shop' where we received a ration of meat each week; one of our secretaries had an unpleasant surprise when she found that hers consisted of several pigs' ears. It was possible to buy sucking-pigs in the outlying villages, and shooting of ducks and geese was allowed in the marshes bordering the Danube, but on the whole we ate the same food in every house. An agreement was made with the French to bring in a small amount of champagne and liqueurs for the Diplomatic shop, to be used for special occasions such as national days, but the most sumptuous meals were at Tito's 'Palace' itself, as when he chose to entertain the diplomats on the occasion of the visit of the President of Poland. The Norwegian Ambassador, who had been in Norway during the German occupation, said that he counted eighty-four sucking-pigs, together with numerous turkeys and chickens, a feast which if held in Norway would have produced a revolution. But there were not many of these receptions, and women were not asked to them . . . was this a relic of Turkish occupation? More common were the parades in the streets, with factory workers carrying banners in honour of Tito and of Stalin; there was never any public recognition of what the Allies had done for them, or of what UNRRA was now trying to do. In the countryside, particularly round Sarajevo, in Bosnia, there was starvation, with no potatoes, no butter, no meat, because of lack of transport and refrigeration, and the Germans having killed all the livestock during the war.

Quite near us in Senjak was a camp of German prisoners, almost all officers; they were made to clean the streets and the steps of the Palace which Tito used for his receptions. In winter they were shivering, in ragged overcoats, sacking and newspapers tied round their legs. They would be pleased if one greeted them. The Yugoslav house-keeper of our Naval Attaché said that it had been a terrible sight when thousands of them were marched into Belgrade, many carrying those who had died on the road.

In October the weather became cold and by Christmas there was thick snow. It drifted through our double windows, and water which we put out for the birds was frozen in fifteen minutes. None of the Embassy cars or even jeeps could reach us, as only main roads were cleared, so we walked into town, taking three-quarters of an hour each way. Our water pipes were frozen and we had to go for baths to some American neighbours, who had managed to find a plumber. Slavka and Magda brought water from them in buckets, heavily wrapped up themselves when the temperature was thirty degrees below zero. It was possible to have an afternoon's ski-ing within a mile of our house, but at Christmas we decided to go with some friends to the village of Planiça in the mountains of Slovenia, where there was a youth club. There were no steep slopes, but ski trails led through pretty forests of pines and birch trees. We kept to ourselves by day but in the evenings the students were friendly and there was even a Christmas tree with a star on it. Someone joked . . . 'was the star of Bethlehem red? . . .'. On Christmas Eve we went to midnight mass in a little church which was crowded with peasants, singing *Heilige Nacht*, the women with bright scarves on their heads. We were driven to it by sleigh, and the driver invited us to his home to meet his family and to wait as we were too early.

Normally, there was little traffic in Belgrade; only

government officials, and the foreigners, had cars or jeeps, the rest used tram-cars. These were crowded for most of the day, but were warm in winter, with a smell of garlic to cheer things up and counter-act that of well-worn boots and sheepskin coats. Crushed together we would go rocking and clanking into town and pour out in the market-place, the *zelini venatz* where fresh fruit and vegetables were sold, and there was a pleasant smell of herbs.

Motor traffic was controlled by police at each main crossroads, who directed it according to the signal given by the drivers with their horns; one 'blow' if they wanted to go straight on, two to go right, and three to go left, a system which worked quite well if only one car approached at a time, but if one gave the wrong signal there was no way to go back on it. As we had no car for the first year, Denis was taken to the office in one of the Embassy jeeps or cars with Jugoslav drivers but after a year some English friends brought out a Hillman for us; this we could only use in Belgrade, as for any trip in the country a jeep or heavy car was needed.

The result of our estrangement from the Jugoslavs, and the smallness of our numbers, meant that we relied for social and recreational entertainment solely on the diplomatic circle. Tennis was played on Embassy courts by British, Belgians, Dutch, French and Americans; shooting was arranged by the Military Attachés; and we had our small lunches and dinner parties with our diplomatic rations. One or two people owned a swimming-pool round which we gathered at weekends in summer. The American Embassy gave a summer dance and the French Embassy a New Year's Eve party. At Christmas our Embassy produced a 'pantomime' – 'Goldilocks and the three Bears' to which only a handful of outsiders, all foreigners, were invited, and we could let ourselves go in fun over the 'broad peoples masses', as Yugoslav newspapers called the communists. The three service attachés were the three bears, the Air Attaché, a jovial type, constantly forgetting his few simple lines. It was held in the Ambassador's drawing-room, where we always found a welcome, and could drop in for a

The British Ambassador and Lady Peake, Belgrade 1948

cup of tea when the office closed. Other occasions for gaiety were farewell parties, when any popular member of our circle was leaving and all sorts of tricks were played, such as putting gold-fish in the victim's water tumbler at dinner, bringing rabbits out of a top-hat, and a sucking-pig to run about the floor among the guests at the time that we were doing a deal with Yugoslavia over bacon, the pig being labelled 'Streaky for Strachey'.

I wrote home . . . "George* has a bowl of gold-fish in his office and John (the Military Attaché) is always teasing them. He pours wine or gin in to see what they will do, and one day got an enormous fish from the market and put it in with them, and George who is very short-sighted did not notice until it was just starting to eat the gold-fish. At the farewell party for him there was gold-fish in his tumbler which he also did not see. When we were having drinks beforehand the pig which

*George Clutton (later Sir) 1st Secretary.

John had bought and kept for two days ran in, and played happily with the rabbit and seven-year-old Benedict Peake was brought down in his dressing-gown to see them. All next week, parties are being given for George, who is clever, amusing and popular. He is going back to London to be head of the Egyptian department. We shall be at seven or eight of them! The only meat one can get now is lamb and you buy them alive in the market-place. A whole one costs five or six pounds. He will have eaten several by the end of the week."

Only the lightest forms of amusement were needed, and we did not indulge in madrigal singing or Scottish dancing, so popular with British communities abroad. Clever members of the Embassy staff, often frustrated with their work with the Jugoslavs, could put their mind to the writing of lyrics for the director of the pantomime. Cicely Ludlam*, who worked with Denis in the commercial department, had a dog called 'Hamlet', who was a constant foil for jokers. In the diplomatic 'bag' from London one day came an artificial tin turd, ordered specially to be put on the carpet in Denis' office; when 'Hamlet' was accused Cicely was in tears, until she tried to clear it up.

After a year, we became tired of Slavka's inquisitive and noisy nature, and of her quarrels with Magda, of whom she became jealous. A young woman called Maritza came in her place, pretty and gentle. Her father had been in France at the beginning of the war and she had had no news of him since; her mother was dead. Her only near relative was her husband, a cheerful young barber, now doing his military service, who would turn up unexpectedly for a few days leave. When he left again she would cry, silently, all day long as she worked. She had been brought up by a kind family called Popovic, now living in the basement of their home and unable to keep her. Maritza was intelligent and discreet; she showed no sign of reporting on our movements and was a thorough, neat worker. Her loyalty to the Popovic family made her critical of the present regime, and once when Denis told her that he had

*Later Lady (Christopher) Mayhew.

been invited to a 'banquet' at the White Palace by Tito she said, with a slight smile, 'What an <u>honour</u> for you!'. She was sorry for Magda and they worked well together, until one day she caught her flirting with her own husband, and then she told us that if we did not dismiss her immediately, she would have to leave herself. Magda went off, saying little, in the black crepe dress which she always wore and old black coat, and Maritza remained. One day she had a telegram saying that her husband was seriously ill in a camp and she went off by train, a journey of several days from which she returned exhausted. At last he was released and started his barber's shop again, but she stayed with us until we left. Afterwards she wrote to me that her father had returned and that she had had a son. She sent a photograph but when, finally, we returned to Belgrade and I made enquiries about her, I was told she had died only a few months before, of heart failure, and that she had often talked of us and hoped to see us once more.

Maritza and her husband were Catholics, and she always wore her crucifix. But the big churches in Belgrade were Orthodox. The largest, the cathedral, was crowded on Sundays, but usually with elderly people. As they entered they would kiss an ikon held by a priest, and he would make the sign of the cross on their foreheads as they dropped a coin into a purse beside him. By the altar several priests in heavy red and gold vestments, one an old man with flowing white hair and beard, sang and waved candles in the half-dark, the ikons dimly lit by flickering electric bulbs. Their voices were rough and wild, and as they sang they would sometimes comb their beards or drink cups of coffee brought by young boys. Some of the congregation were so poor that they were wearing only summer sandals over thick socks in the winter. Once, at Easter, I watched a mother with a small boy of about four years, who put a little toy tank on the floor inside the church and began pushing it round. His mother bought some candles from the man at the door and put them in a tray of sand, then went up to the altar. The little boy raced up behind her making a noise with his boots and a priest came from behind the altar to speak angrily to him, so that his mother took away the tank and put it in her hand-bag. She made him cross himself and kiss a book on the altar, then gave him back the tank and he went off happily, pushing it all over the floor among other people. The church was attractively gaudy, the tall hats of the priests and the candles and ikons making it look like something from the Old Testament, while outside, rather incongruously, were the graves of some partisan soldiers with the Red Star over them.

Travelling in the countryside was not restricted except by the poor and sometimes dangerous condition of the roads and bridges after the war. We were able to drive to the Adriatic coast to stay with our consul in Split, and also to visit Skoplje, travelling there by train and then borrowing the consular jeep in order to reach Lake Ochrid near the Albanian border. The road was rough and mountainous; it was November and there was snow in places. We reached the town of Ochrid after dark, only to find that the passes we had obtained in Belgrade counted for nothing, and instead of seeing three of the finest churches and spending a day by the lake, we were apparently under arrest and told to leave immediately, which would have meant another six-hour drive on the precipitous roads, with a tired chauffeur. Denis insisted on seeing one church in the dark while I sat by an old iron stove to keep warm, and we eventually left at 9 a.m. the next morning pursued by a soldier on a motor bicycle who followed us for six miles. We had been accompanied everywhere by a polite young officer, wearing an old 'British warm' overcoat, but he could not understand our innocent desire to see the early Christian churches of Ochrid. We caught a glimpse of the lake, surrounded by snowcapped mountains, and it snowed hard as we returned to Skoplje so that I was glad of a fleece-lined coat which had been left at the consulate by our military mission during the war, to protect me in the open jeep. On our way we met peasants in striking costumes, and nomads called Vlachs in heavily embroidered black dresses, with coins and beads in their hair, and small blue crosses tattooed on their foreheads between the eyes to show they were Christians, a habit they have kept since Turkish rule. They were leading their horses down a steep mountain pass, with elaborate silver harness and embroidered cloths on their saddles. Visiting Ochrid years later, and arriving by plane, it was difficult to realise that it was the same place, with the churches proudly displayed to tourists, and a huge lake-side hotel provided for the holidays of factory workers.

In June 1948 there were dramatic events in Belgrade, when after much bickering Stalin had broken his 'friendly' relations with Tito, who refused to dismiss some of his senior ministers whom the Russians insisted were 'tools of the West'. There was secret rejoicing among all 'westerners' and it gave us a feeling of hope for the country and more interest in its future. However, a few months later Denis was summoned back to London, as he had been appointed consul in Chicago. We were given some of the typical 'send-off' parties ourselves. It would all be a strange contrast and once more we were sad to leave, both Belgrade, our household, and the little group which our much-loved friends, the British Ambassador and his wife, called 'the family'.

Slavka, our Communist maid.

89

Chapter Nine

The Windy City, 1949–51

A vivid recollection of Chicago is of the snow whirling round the tall Palmolive Buildings near our flat. Arriving in January, we soon had experience of the winds which caught one at every street corner, snow was piled high on each side of the roads, partly by the snow ploughs which drove a narrow strip down the centre for essential traffic. But private cars were shapeless mounds parked in front of the buildings, stranded for days and sometimes weeks. It was as quiet as Belgrade in winter, no motor-horns, no trambells ringing, no sound of pedestrian feet on the side-walks; only the sleighbells of Roumania were missing. The blizzards filled the air with snow, through which the neon signs on high buildings shone at night, and the golden light from office windows in the late afternoon. The lake was frozen round the edges in huge blocks which looked as though they had been tossed onto the beaches from passing ships.

Chicago, with its suburbs, extended for twenty-five miles along the shores of Lake Michigan. It was the sixth largest city in the world. We were soon swept into it's busy life, as Denis was the Consul in charge of promoting British trade with the United States, one of several 'Trade Consuls' spread throughout the country. The British Consulate in Chicago had a large staff, and was situated in the 'Loop' area, so called because of an old overhead railway which used to circle round it.

In contrast to Belgrade we saw very little of the foreign

Consular corps. There were few official occasions to which they were all invited as a body, though the French, Dutch, Italian and Swiss would appear at social gatherings and at the clubs . . . such as the 'Tavern', half-way up a tall skyscraper building . . . frequented by business-men. We ourselves were privileged to be members of the 'Saddle and Cycle' on Chicago's smart Near North Side, where we could play tennis, swim or dine, and though we were not enthusiasts for club life, it was a haven of well kept grounds, good food and good company not far from our flat on busy Michigan Avenue.

Among our friends in the consular corps were the Turkish Consul-General, Hikmet Anli and his wife, Sema, who had been in the Turkish Embassy in London during the war, while we were in Turkey. Their last post had been Delhi, and I found that Sema and I looked at America with the same eyes. For both of us the cost of living was extremely high. We went shopping together, or more often only window-shopping in the big stores, Marshall Fields and Carson, Pirie Scott, taking the bus down Michigan Avenue, and having our lunch in one of the clean and efficient drug-stores on the way.

Sema found that they were the only people in their large apartment block who did not take a certain brand of milk. Every few weeks she was called upon by a pleasant young man, who she realised would get a large prize if he could win the whole block for his firm. But she said to him "We are Turks. Don't you know that they are very obstinate people. The more you ask them to do something, the more they refuse". They had a cup of coffee together, drinking his rival's milk. We were both intrigued by American business enterprise, such as the laundries sending brand new articles to replace any lost, in order to keep one's custom.

Neither Sema nor I cared for the 'Ladies Lunches' so popular with leisured American women, preferring small gatherings in our own apartments. We were lucky enough, in ours, to have the services of a black maid called Mattie, whose continued employment was the condition of our tenancy being accepted. Mattie was a dignified middle-aged woman who had been a children's nurse until theories that they should do anything they pleased made it too much of a responsibility for her, and she became an excellent cook and maid. She had been brought up in the South, and now longed to visit Paris, as she heard that the French treated negroes as equals. She spoke of her ancestors in Africa as 'those old people with rings in their noses', and she had never married because, she said, so many of her women friends were tied to 'no-good men' who drank and were out of work, the fate of many negroes in the slums of Chicago. She had a soft, musical voice and would chuckle when Denis teased her, or asked her to tell us stories of the gangsters in the 'bad old days', in which she inferred that our landlord had played some part; but she talked bitterly of the rigging of local elections against the negroes, and when we wanted to invite a negro professor to one of our parties she said the rules of the building were such that he would have to come up in the service lift.

In spite of the enormous mixture of races which made up the population of Chicago, we seldom met other than the Anglo-Saxons in social and business circles. There were any number of societies, from the Daughters of the American Revolution and the Daughters of the British Empire to the Ulster Society, the Burns Society, and the more serious Civil Rights Association and Council on Foreign Relations, all of whose functions we attended from time to time. Our only contact with Jugoslavia was when we discovered an Orthodox monastery near a town appropriately named Libertyville, where a priest was helping refugees who had made their escape, and when the Serbian community, mostly workers in the steel mills of Gary, Indiana, held a rally in a Chicago Hotel which was addressed by ex-King Peter.

A more surprising discovery was a community of Assyrians, centred round their patriarch, Mar Shimun the Twenty-third, who had been in exile since the end of the British mandate in Iraq in 1932. He was an imposing figure with a black beard cut in Assyrian fashion, and he made visits to the consulate in connection with his residence permit. He held the title

'Beatitude' and also 'Holiness' but he felt that the latter might offend the Irish Roman Catholics who held office in the municipality under Mayor Daly, and that they were prejudiced against him. We invited him to our flat on various occasions, when he drank only lemonade, and were in turn invited to the thirtieth anniversary of his enthronement, when his Chicago parishioners gave him a Buick car 'to replace the ten-year-old conveyance in which he has travelled from Atlantic to Pacific'. There were three hundred guests on one of the hottest days of the year in the small meeting-hall, but an old priest courteously attended us and showed us the few old manuscripts and relics which they had managed to save from destruction after their exile.

Although Chicago had the reputation of being isolationist in world affairs and particularly anti-British, the only sign of it was in the daily paper, the 'Chicago Tribune', which published insulting editorials headed 'Britain jumps to the crack of the whip', 'Mr Attlee compliments Mr Stalin', and 'The enemy within our gates' which listed 'Organisations for international peace' such as the Chicago Council on Foreign Relations, the English-Speaking Union, the American Association for the United Nations who were all supposed to have as their evil object the further involvement of America in world affairs. American Rhodes' scholars at one time came under fire as being British agents . . . 'Rhodes' ideals shape U.S. policies', 'Pro-British scholars in key posts'. There were cartoons of John Bull begging from America and trading with China, of Truman on his knees surrendering the keys of the U.S. treasury to John Bull on the anniversary of the surrender of Cornwallis at Yorktown, and money being handed on to Asian communists. When a picture appeared of John Bull with a wooden leg begging for alms, and on receiving them, taking off his wooden leg and running away on two good ones, a courteous old gentleman telephoned the Consulate to apologise 'on the part of all decent Americans'; Denis happened to take the call and he became one of our best friends whom we often met at his club, where he talked of his work in Palestine as a missionary, and of the British he knew there.

This was also the era of 'McCarthyism' in Washington and all over the country; among members of Chicago's two big Universities, Chicago and North Western, we encountered the bitterness they felt as it particularly affected the teaching profession.

The reporters working for the 'Chicago Tribune' were of high quality, and one, a girl, was often partnered by Denis at the 'Saddle and Cycle' Club tennis matches and together they won the mixed doubles handicap; but we regarded Colonel McCormick, the owner of the paper, as our arch-enemy. He lived in one of the expensive suburbs of the town, where he occasionally entertained our Consul-General, Berkeley Gage. They were products of the same prep-school in England, but whereas the Colonel, for some reason of his own, took the line that Britain, particularly under the Socialist government which we had at that moment, was 'going to the dogs', Berkeley was always a optimist, with humanity, good looks and good humour. He was a popular figure who raised the whole morale of the Consulate on his arrival, as successor to someone whose sole interests had been bridge and golf. Berkeley was descended from the General Gage of the Battle of Bunker Hill, and his mother had been American. With his two dogs, his Dutch valet and his Bentley car – for which he was nick-named 'Bentley Gage' – he was just the sort of Englishman the Colonel admired. Denis did not expect very much from their friendship, but after a good dinner in the McCormick mansion, and receiving the admiring attentions of the Colonel's daughter, Alice, Berkeley always hoped that the tone of the editorials would change.

The real confrontation came on the unusual occasion of a Chinese wedding. The bride was the daughter of K. C. Wu, governor of Formosa and formerly mayor of Shanghai known to the Colonel and to Berkeley, who had served in China. In order to be married, the bridegroom had to be baptised, and chose the names of his two friends. The question was, whose

95

should come first, but the Colonel won, and the bridegroom became 'Rutherford Berkeley Yu'.

Berkeley disliked making speeches, and had one written in general terms which he used in different places under different titles; but his gregarious instinct won his audiences. He would not notice if a person were black, yellow or white, and a negro workman who had helped him with his car when it broke down would be asked back to his flat for a drink along with anyone else whom he might have asked at the same time.

For his work, Denis had to travel in fourteen states, meeting businessmen through the Chambers of Commerce, Rotary Clubs, Lion Clubs, Kiwanis and others and being interviewed by the press and on television. Many people whom he met paid us return visits in Chicago. After a short spring, when the cold winds turned to fresh breezes down Michigan Avenue, the summer set in and temperatures rose to ninety degrees. The smell of the stockyards hung over the town, and people from the crowded slums of the west side came to the Lake to sit on its stony shore and get a breath of fresh air cooled by the water. In our flat was a set of books, beautifully bound and published by the Lakeside Press of Chicago, which contained the memoirs and diaries of some of the early settlers in America. It was difficult to recognise in this huge city the small trading post it had been in the early nineteenth century, but when we left it to travel in our English car first to the East and then the West, the experiences of these people became more real. It must have comforted the Pilgrim Fathers, after the trials of their sea voyage, to land in a part of America so much resembling England and its flora and fauna, as New England, just as, later, many Swedes were to settle near the pine forests of Minnesota.

After an invigorating swim in the Atlantic with a Russian friend, Serge Chermayeff, his English wife, two sons and an Airdale dog, and lunch with them in their holiday home in Cape Cod, we spent several days with our old American friend, Bobby Dunn, in Katonah, New York State. We had first met him in Turkey during the war, when, as Assistant Naval Attaché at the American Embassy in Ankara, he had come to Trebizond on some secret mission, and of all the visitors we had there, he was the most interesting. As a young man he had taken part in the gold rush in the Yukon in 1898, and had made the first ascent of Mount Wrangel in Alaska. He had been a journalist in five wars, and won the highest American award for his first-hand reporting of the Battle of the Somme. In both World Wars he was an intelligence officer working closely with the British, and he knew London well, but his favourite pastimes, when free, were mountain-climbing, trekking and camping.

Now, aged seventy-three, he was living with his sister in an old house filled with family treasures and momentoes of his travels. It was cool, even though the temperature was in the nineties; Bobby disliked 'modern gadgets' like air-conditioning, refrigerators and television. His main interest was the garden, filled with phlox and roses, the latter being attacked by pests on which he waged constant war. Wearing only a torn shirt, a pair of nylon shorts, Indian sandals and a cotton hat soaked in water on his head, he paced the garden armed with a spray and followed by his Chow dog. In the cool of the evening, when I had gone to bed, he took Denis on a tour of local bars, guiding him home with difficulty in our car in the early hours of the morning.

He arranged for us to meet several of his friends at lunch and at dinner, where there was lively talk and argument on politics, and we visited the home of Roosevelt at Hyde Park, then open to the public, who could see his grave in the garden. Bobby wore a loose-fitting tropical suit and a large Mexican straw hat, and carried a fly-whisk. On the steps of the front-door stood a vacuum cleaner, a schoolgirl gazing at it in wonder. 'What do you think that's for?' said Bobby, 'To smoke out rats? That's it . . . to smoke out Republican rats . . .'

We were invited to tea by one of his neighbours, in their large country-house, in the slave-quarters of which were living the Empress Zita of Hapsburg and her daughter,

Archduchess Charlotte. We happened to have with us a Jugoslav friend who was visiting Washington, who had joined us with Bobby, and he gazed with amused interest at the young girl whose family had once ruled his country, when she joined us for tea, unaware that he was a member of the new régime. Driving to the West in the following year, we stopped in Taos, New Mexico to call on Frieda, widow of D. H. Lawrence. We were guided to the house by finding one of her neighbours, the Hon. Dorothy Brett, living nearby with the Esher coat-of-arms painted on her garage door. She was at her easel, busy with a scene from Indian dancing, dressed in blue jeans and wearing an old pair of spectacles with cracked lenses. Freida lived less than a mile away and invited us into a large, cool room in the adobe house, hung with Lawrences' early paintings. She talked about world affairs, but when there was a crash of thunder overhead, said quickly, 'Do you think there is going to be another war?' She said that Lawrence had always worked easily, and would stop writing from time to time to do some cooking, or to trim a hat for her.

The only buildings which stands out in my memory of that trip is Brown's Hotel in Denver, famous in gold-rush days, and the shaky houses of Virginia City, a 'ghost town' of the same period, where we stayed in quaint, dilapidated lodgings and were introduced by the lady owner to all the local characters in the town's only bar, including the garbage man. It had no local industry now and had become an artists colony, with one excellent restaurant. Towns and small-towns – what we would call villages – were less memorable than the countryside, the huge plains, the Rocky Mountains, and even desert; most of all the weird, moonlike landscape of the Grand Canyon. We had not imagined the vastness of the country, and the fact that when leaving the great highways for desert or mountain tracks, people were warned to take water with them in summer, even in some cases on the highways themselves.

Back in Chicago the time passed quickly until we were due to sail on home leave, with presents of food, nylons stockings and other luxuries for our families. We joined the boat in New York on Denis' fortieth birthday, and found a telegram waiting for us on board . . .

Bon voyage to Iona and you
Birthday greetings and may it come true
That whatever the winds, be they trade or trailing,
Through the roaring forties you'll have smooth sailing . . .
Chicago Consular Staff.

.

Painting by the Karaj River, Iran

We had two spells in London, one between 1951 and 1953, and another between 1955 and 1959. In December 1953 Denis was sent to open the Embassy in Tehran after the fall of Moussadeq, and 2 months later I travelled out by train, ship and bus with Rachel Franks, the wife of one of Denis' staff.

Chapter Ten

Letters from Baghdad and Tehran, 1954–55

Baghdad   February, 1954

Here we are in Baghdad! It does not seem much further to Tehran compared with the distance we have already come, providing we can get on the 'plane, which only goes once a week.

It is really eastern here, with Arabs all in Biblical dress, palm trees, and the house I am staying in is an old Turkish one right on the banks of the Tigris, a very wide, muddy river. It is like being in Turkey again.

The bus-ride from Beirut was quite an adventure. It is a large sort of aluminium charabanc, pulled by a diesel motor, with comfortable seats for about thirty passengers, and a big luggage compartment which easily took all my luggage. We left Beirut in warm sunny weather at midday, and drove to Damascus in a smaller bus, right over the coastal mountain range of the Lebanon, reaching Damascus at about 3 p.m. We could not see much of the town as the bus station was outside it, also it was raining slightly. About two hours later we got into the bus for Baghdad and set off across the desert, which was not sand so much as yellow mud. The drivers go by instinct as there is no road, and when the night is clear, as it usually is, they are guided by the stars. It rained heavily and we were nearly stuck several times (and we heard later that

101

the bus was sometimes stuck for several days), but we stopped at a little shack after a time, to have tea, and were given boxes of sandwiches and fruit to eat for supper as we went along. Owing to the weather we were about four hours late in reaching Baghdad, but we slept well, and Rachel's children were very good. When we stopped for an early morning cup of tea, the door of the bus was opened by an Arab garage-hand in flowing robes, and David, who is five, said "Look, Mummy, there's Jesus!"

Yesterday I was invited to a party at the Embassy. The house is a large white one with green shutters, on the banks of the river and with palm trees all round; a tame gazelle tied to one of them. It is cool inside with a small pool in the hall, the first I have seen but they are usual here. Most people I talked to had seen Denis on his way through in December.

Tehran   February, 1954

I miss England. I was looking at the trees outside the window and there is an oak which reminds me of it. Everyone likes Teheran, apparently, far the best of the Middle East posts, and from what I have seen of it, it has clean broad streets and interesting antique shops, and a lovely position under a huge range of snow-covered mountains. We had to stay an extra day in Baghdad because the 'plane could not fly on the day we should have left, owing to a snow storm in Teheran – but we arrived yesterday at ten o'clock after an interesting flight over the desert. Denis and Rachel's husband could not meet us because they had to go with Roger* to present his credentials to the Shah, but they were back at about eleven o'clock, all in uniform to the delight of the children!

Our house is large and Victorian in style, rather like a vicarage. The furnishing is not bad, comfortable chairs with cretonne covers, and the floors, except for the sitting-room which is parquet, are tiled with blue Persian tiles. It

*Roger and Constance Stevens were our Ambassador and Ambassadress, we had known them for a long time.

will be improved when we have some pictures.
The air, and the height, make you very sleepy...

March, 1954

Denis had been called back to London before the opening of
the oil talks here. At least we have had a week together, and I
shall be able to unpack while he is away. All my baggage has
arrived except, unfortunately, my ski-boots which I stupidly
packed in the trunk which will not be here until April This
week I borrowed some and we went out for half a day to the
nearest slopes, and on this Sunday will go again.

It is fun here. Constance and I have been about a bit together,
calling on other ambassadresses. This morning we went to the
Indian, a nice oldish woman (though it is difficult to tell an
Indian's age) in a pretty sari, under a large picture of Gandhi
in a silver frame. Yesterday we went to the Russian, she had
been in Belgrade when I was there so that I could talk to her a
little in Serbian. On Tuesday night we went to the largest dinner
party I have ever seen, given by the Persian Foreign Minister
for Roger and Constance and some departing diplomats. There
were no speeches, it was all pleasant and beautifully organised,
the food was marvellous and there were fifty-two people, all
seated! It was in an immense room, everyone in evening dress
and the Persians and other Easterners there had lovely clothes
often in their national materials, embroidered, and with lots
of jewellery. Persians have olive skins and black hair rather
like Italians, many have lovely heads and necks, and huge
dark eyes. As we sat at the table about forty waiters in white
gloves advanced, first with the soup, then fish, then dishes of
meat and rice, then ice-cream. The table was about fifty yards
long, with a strip of Persian embroidery down the centre, and
tall glass chandeliers instead of silver ones.

In our 'compound' the Residence is in the middle with its
gardens, garages, laundry, etc., and the houses of the staff are
all round, with gardens separated by hedges. None of the
hedges are out yet, not being evergreen, so we all seem to be
in the same garden, but forsythia and violets are budding now.

The Residence greenhouse is full of cinerarias, and we have a greenhouse too, but it has got to have the roof mended.

Gulhak   July, 1955
We are now up in the summer Residence, as the Stevens are on leave. It is far cooler and very nice. At the moment we have hardly any furniture as new things are due from England, instead of bringing it all up from Tehran as they used to do, but it is quite pleasant just camping-out, in country-cottage style, and as many people have gone on leave there is not a lot of entertaining to do. Our cat is getting used to it now. We brought him up by car, following the Embassy lorry with our suitcases, china, glass, candlesticks, etc., and he howled all the way, with his ears back. For two days he crept about the new house sniffing everything, but now he follows me round and yesterday went to sleep in a suitcase that I was unpacking.

This is a real old-style Persian house for the summer, with big verandahs front and back and all the rooms opening onto them. We have our carpet and furniture on the verandahs and leave them all the time and entertain there as well as using them ourselves all day. One of the best moments is breakfast in the early morning. The garden has a nice lawn and flower-beds and a blue-tiled pool, oleanders on the verandah steps, lavender and zinneas in the beds below. And huge trees called Asiatic planes are all round the house to give shade; they are very tall, with leaves high up to give an umbrella effect. There are nightingales here in May, before we came up, but now there are golden orioles in the pine trees among the planes.

There is just one large bedroom upstairs, and a dressing-room, and bathroom reached by an outdoor staircase, up which water was carried for the bath before it was laid on in pipes. The verandahs, back and front, are as big as the room itself, so that no sun can get in the windows, always open to get a 'through draught'. The kitchen is quite a long way off, in the garden, because entertaining is often done in a large tent on the lawn, the dining room being quite small.

In May 1953 we spent a few days with Chicago friends in Venice where Tony Kendall was the Consul.

Chapter Eleven

Langouste or Langui.
Venice, 1953

May, 1953

We came to Venice about tea-time with our friends, who were installed in a tourist hotel while we went to the Consulate, also on the Grand Canal. Our room was on the lower floor of the old Palazzo, dilapidated but still elegant, and we could hear the water lapping just below the window and see the prows of the gondolas passing, followed by the top half of the gondolier, sometimes wearing his summer straw hat with ribbons floating behind, though it was still cold weather, in early May.

The Kendalls inhabited, chiefly, the main floor of the Palazzo, four or five immense rooms with marble floors, and marble walls hung with huge oil paintings; but not over-furnished, except, it seemed at first sight, for chairs, of which there were about twenty grouped in the main living-room round tables of varying sizes. Charlie the fox terrier played about, looking for imaginary mice at the bottom of the curtain which divided the room in half for warmth and made it look less like an audience chamber.

Mila Kendall showed us our bathroom, downstairs on the level of our room, equipped with a modern geyser, "but," she aid, "silly thing, hot water do not come, you must wait, and turn, turn and turn, I don't know what is with it . . . Sometimes," she pointed to the lavatory, "it come here . . .". Our room was high and spacious too, with a polished wooden floor and three steps up to a table and chair by the window. The walls were hung with printed linen, like an 'arras', behind which one felt might be hidden a courtesan, or murderer.

At the same time the Caccias from Vienna were in Venice on holiday, and the Kendalls went out to supper with them, when they asked Mila if she could get for them a certain sort of fish to take back to Vienna for a banquet. We met later in a bar, with our American friends, who had been luxuriating in their bath-room with good plumbing after several weeks in Yugoslavia, Turkey and Greece, but who were already looking at Venice with half a mind, the other half running on to Florence, Pisa, Ravenna . . . We decided to stay with the Kendalls for a few days, as they urged us to.

The next morning we went to the fish market with Mila, in the Consulate motor-boat, calling for benzine on the way. We lay anchored in a quiet backwater of the Canal, while the 'motor-man' disappeared. "He is devil" said Mila, "He make me all sort of trouble. Why he not go earlier for benzine? Why he not have ticket? They will not give him. He is lazy like nothing! We tell him . . . Wear uniform, when Ambassador (Caccia) come . . . he not wear; they are all same; not want to look like servant . . ."

We sat on in the morning sun. There was suddenly a banging above our heads, on one of the many balconies, loaded with potted plants, which over-hung the Canal. "Now they beat carpets on us" said Mila, "That is nice. He make us nice trouble, that devil." The man came back and we went on without incident, but at the fish market, by the time our purchases were made, the boat was hemmed in by a number of gondolas and barges discharging market goods. In backing through them, the motor went wrong; after sitting for some time, while bargees and passers-by offered advice, jumping to and fro between our boat and the canal side strip of pavement, Mila decided we should take a 'water-bus'.

"Only well we not in middle canal," she said, "we wait long

106

time before they sent motor-boat taxi to pick us".

Once aboard the 'bus' we found ourselves sitting back to back with our fellow travellers who were on a sight-seeing tour on their own. Later on we all dined with the Caccias, when Mila asked Lady Caccia again what fish she had wanted, and Tony said, "Mila, have you not done anything about it yet?" Mila said, "No, because I not sure – You want these snake-fishes, Lady Caccia, like eel?" Lady Caccia said, "No, I want langouste, the cray-fish, they are especially good here . . ."

"Ah!" Mila said, "I thought you mean 'langui' – same name nearly!" We all laughed. Tony said, "That's it, Mila, you get them ten kilos of snake-fish . . . ten yards of snake-fish!"

On the way home, lingering in the narrow streets and looking in the still lighted windows of the luxury shops, Mila continued . . . "Well I not send ten kilo 'langui' to Vienna. Lady Caccia say . . . "I want it, very nice cold on table, look nice for 'buffet'. I think . . . how she want this snake-fish? Nobody eat in Venice; this is cheapest fish, live on filth, really, *anybody* take it from Canal. *Now* I know, *now* I laugh . . . !"

Denis went to Ethiopia as an Ambassador in December 1959. We travelled there by ship from Marseilles to Djibouti and then by train to Addis Abeba.

Chapter Twelve

Memories of 'Addis', 1960–62

... the cool early morning with the mist below the house, over the 'Ladies Mile' ... Abdulla rushing in with breakfast and spilling the tea into the tea-cosy ... Denis walking off down the drive to the office after listening to the nine o'clock news ... and Gabre Mariam, the groom, bringing 'Whisky' to the door, for me to go riding with Betty and Ann. Trotting through the tukuls and out onto the plain, deciding who would gallop and who would go slowly ... discussing our horses and their ways, and gossiping a bit. Coffee with Ann, or Betty, or with Pamela Parker on the way home, or straight back in order to go shopping.

Taking Sayid down with me to watch the open Ford while I shopped, and to ward off the beggars. Going down the main street and back another way ... perhaps going to the dressmakers and finding her out, as one never exactly kept appointments, neither she nor her clients; if in, she usually would have a Greek air hostess of Ethiopian Air-lines who would translate for me.

Drinks in the garden on the swing seat before lunch, with the Peels from the Consul's house next door wandering over to join us, or going over to them where they sat under a big tree and Warbishet, their house-boy, scurried in and out with bare feet, carrying tonic water and beer ... Michèle Peel coming back from school in the landrover. Lunch alone, or a lunch party with Fiterari gliding round . . . Schifferaw very poised and correct . . . Abdulla still rushing and panting, and Sayid, when on duty too, very decorously bending as he served one, and holding his head very straight on his slender neck as he walked.

Into the kitchen later if there was a dinner party, to see how it was going . . . Aderai and Ergete hard at work. Sometimes the dhobi's elegant and lazy son was standing by the kitchen door doing nothing, no-one taking any notice of him, the dhobi himself smiling and bowing ingratiatingly if one happened to run into him. Then to see Moussa in the garden about planting out seedlings. "Come, come," he would say to each flower that was not yet out, or "die . . . yes, die" of those that had finished; and "no die . . . come, come very good" of those which would flower after the rains. He would touch his round white crocheted cap (he is a Moslem) roguishly as I went off, and give a charming wry smile on account of his hare-lip. With his little goatee beard and lively eyes, he was the most attractive of the servants.

A rest perhaps for one hour, until the gardeners began to use the tap outside the bedroom window to fill their cans one after another. Into the big sitting-room, or Denis' small study if colder than usual, for a cup of tea and biscuit or cake. Denis coming up from the office at five o'clock, and the horses brought for a ride. 'Gida' and 'Whisky' waiting quietly at the bottom of the steps, with Gabre Mariam, bare-footed and blue felt cap in hand, waiting to see whether he was to come with us or not. If I did not go he would ride 'Whisky', or sometimes another of the grooms would come, riding behind. If we both went out they would wait on the terrace below the flag-pole, watching for us to come up with the drive or down from the hill behind the house.

We would ride to meet Ewen at his house, and Micky or Derek at theirs, and then usually turn up the hill . . . our favourite ride but not theirs because there was too much walking, up and down, and not enough galloping. If one went

'Gida' and 'Whisky'

to the 'Ladies Mile', Ewen and Micky would race, and sometimes I would too, but Denis would school 'Gida' to a canter and then gallop separately as he was so powerful and full of spirits.

Up on the hill there were wonderful views all round as we climbed, over the whole town, the plains and hills to the south, and the Entoto range behind (although we were on a spur of it); all a rich blue-green-grey colour from the eucalyptus and pine forests and the smoke from the tukuls hidden among them, a Corot-like colour, but with patches of red or grey earth nearer to us on the path. It would be a very stony path to walk up, but there were always country people climbing cheerfully or doggedly on foot, who would answer Ewen's greetings in Amharic with surprise and pleasure.

At the top were brambles and briars and thorn trees, and patches of ploughed earth guarded by fiercely barking dogs, but there was one clear grass track which the horses loved, going faster and faster until they swerved up a light mound to the ruins of an old rock church, where we stopped to rest. We sometimes made a short round, along an old Italian road, now grass-grown, where birds fluttered and chirped in the bushes, and then on our way down, after six o'clock, it would grow dark and lights would come on in the town. In the distance the plum-pudding-like hill of Managasha would be outlined in the sunset, and other hills, stretching away behind it.

After the ride we all separated, Denis drank his favourite fresh lime juice while having a bath and changing, and we would go to the little sitting-room, if we were alone for the evening, or I would go and check the table decorations, and Denis the seating arrangements, if we had a dinner-party. At 7.15 p.m. it would be time to change again and at 7.30 p.m. the fire would be lit in the big sitting-room and Fiterari would assemble the drinks in the passage under the archway. As I came out dressed at 8 p.m., our dhobi, or the Joys' dhobi, was standing at the front door ready to open it, and I waited for the guests by the fire. Dinner parties usually went on only till

11 or 11.30 p.m., and then any of our own staff who had been invited too would stay on to chat a few minutes before walking down the hill to their homes. The 'boys' would wait to close the front door and take away all the glasses. We would go to bed, and sometimes hear the hyenas which prowled in the servants 'village' behind, or sometimes just the scuffling of the guard as it did its night patrol round the house. Through the windows on the little courtyard in the centre of the house, open to the sky, one could see the moon over the giant eucalyptus on the hill.

Iona with The Emperor, Haile Selassie, at a Red Cross Bazaar

Chapter Thirteen

The 'Coup D'Etat'
Addis Ababa December 1960

This morning I woke up thinking, "Really I must tell Abdulla to be quieter when he brings in the breakfast". Abdulla is always in a hurry, on very flat feet, banging doors – but this morning it was more than usual. His knock came on our door, at 7 a.m. instead of our usual breakfast hour of eight. "Dedjajdmatch Asrate Kassa, Sir" he said. Denis scrambled out of bed not knowing what this could mean. A high-placed relative of the Royal family calling at 7 a.m. He vanished in his dressing-gown, and I drowsed on for twenty minutes or so. Then back he came, "There has been a 'Coup' – the Crown Prince is under arrest by the Imperial Bodyguard, all the Ministers too, only Asrate Kassa and the Minister of Education have escaped so far. They came here to ask me to send a message to the Emperor."

The Emperor is now in Brazil, and this time has been especially chosen. Denis went off to the office and I leant out of the window and saw Asrate Kassa, an impressive figure, huddled in a small sort of mini car with another Ethiopian, glide off down the drive to possible arrest themselves, but they had done all they could. I had breakfast. An American wandered in to find us and tell us the news, which he too had heard. Our wireless operators were getting through to London. The day passed slowly, with rumours first that only Denis

115

could leave the compound, then I found that other wives had gone out shopping. My mother-in-law who was staying with us was perturbed, though outwardly calm, at a situation she had never been in before. Sir Harry Luke, seventy-six years old and also our guest, was full of life and interest. After I had given some uncertain instructions to the cook as to what sort of meals to prepare in this emergency (we had invited twenty people to dinner, but as telephones were all cut we had no means of communicating with them) We all sat in the garden reading recent English newspapers. It was a beautiful, sunny day, with a light wind. We gazed at the distant hills, and listened to aeroplanes droning above. All commercial airlines had stopped flying, so we could only conjecture what these planes could be. From time to time the internal compound telephone rang and I was fetched to hear arrangements for staff living outside to be brought in, and the possibility of the British colony having to come in also. Wireless transmitters were brought in from the office, and the Military Attaché brought some arms into the cellar. All through the day we listened to news broadcasts, but at 7 p.m. only, it was announced from London that the Crown Prince had taken over from the Emperor. Here, at 1 p.m. his message to the Ethiopians was broadcast, forced on him by the Bodyguard. It sounded flat and mechanical.

Our Sudanese guards, of whom we have fifteen, were dispersed round the compound with rifles. Armed police were on the gate instead of them, sent by the Ethiopians. Sir Harry, my mother-in-law and I went shopping in the afternoon, flying the flag on the car as I do not usually do. We bought some fish, fruit and vegetables, and called for my coat at the cleaners. The town looked much the same except for the guards at the Post Office and banks, and several armoured cars by the Palace. All day Ambassadors and other foreign representatives were driving about visiting each other, owing to the telephones being cut. They often met in the street, the Ambassadors recognising each other's flags, and when they passed the person they were going to call on, they got out and talked where they were. At 5 p.m. the assistant chief of Protocol arrived at the Residence in an army jeep and said that he wanted Denis to go with him, after we had asked him if there would be a curfew. At 7 p.m. he said, so we knew none of our original guests could come, though the Yugoslav Embassy had sent someone up to enquire about it.

Instead, we had eight of the Embassy staff, four of them from outside, but being housed in the compound for the night, plus their children in tents. During dinner, which was disjointed owing to the servants being upset as well as us, the men went to listen to the news, more declarations by the Crown Prince – eleven points of a new programme read out by the usual radio announcer. We dispersed at eleven o'clock, the men again to the office to send more telegrams to London. We women talked on general matters, but also of Asrate Kassa and what might have happened to him and many others, during the day, and of how the English couple who ran a school for the Emperor's grandchildren, were faring.

The next morning we woke as usual to the sound of pigeons coo-ing, and of the gardeners filling their watering cans. My mother-in-law and I went out and sat in the garden after being told that we could not go into town without the chauffeur, and Denis needed him to go to a meeting of Ambassadors. Towards the end of the morning Ann Joy rang up, to say that she had driven down to shop herself, but that there was so little left in the shops and the grocers were all exhausted and terrified, and the market was running out of vegetables, that it would be wise to get all one could as soon as possible. Denis said I could have the car at a quarter to three, and my mother-in-law got ready to come with me. By twenty-five minutes to three the cook had not come back from his lunch and I wanted him to come with me to buy a stock of potatoes and sugar. I went to the back door and asked the second cook to go and find him. At that moment there was a dull rumble. I did not think it was thunder, as some people did. Then there was a sharp crackling noise, and Abdulla appeared, his large eyes very wide, and said, "Trouble, I think, Memsahib". By the time

I had gone to the front of the house there was continuous firing, and so it went on until 5.30 p.m. At three o'clock Nellie Eaden came up with a car-load of children who played round the house so that they could come in quickly if necessary. Bullets hit the chancery where Denis and the rest of the men were working, but did not reach the top of the compounds where our house is.

It was the day for the Embassy shop so the wives opened it as usual at 4 p.m. and the children came into our house for a drink and some biscuits. They had just begun running out again when there was a deafening whistle from jet planes passing right over us. They were all terrified for a moment and I thought we should go to the cellar, but it meant crossing a small courtyard so we hesitated, also the light was cut off and the cellar would be pitch dark. Nothing more came, and the firing continued down in the town. The smaller children recovered, quicker than the older ones. Andrew Joy, aged five, said cheerfully, "There was a big noise and then I had *another* lemonade!" We had three of the Sudanese guards on the steps with their rifles. Several of them at the gate had had to stop people trying to get in, before the Ethiopian police arrived, but eighteen British were allowed in to take refuge. We had some tea, groups of us in different houses, and eventually at 6 p.m. when all seemed quiet the children were taken home, but two families living in flimsy bungalows near the gate were housed higher up in stone buildings. Several of the servants' families came into our kitchen and pantry but I told them they were no safer than in their own 'tukeuls', and Ewen Fergusson turned about fifty out of the stables where the horses might have taken fright and trampled on them.

We heard on the news at 7 p.m. that the Emperor was coming back, but no-one knew when, or where he would land, and was not likely to say if they did know. The fighting had been between the rebel Bodyguard, his 'crack' soldiers, and the Army who were loyal, and chiefly took place by the divisional headquarters of the Army near the railway and to the south of the town. Luckily the Air Force remained loyal too and kept quiet; if they had come in *we* were very much on their route. We thought they might come to the help of the Army headquarters but we could only see a few planes cruising over the town in the early evening, backwards and forwards like huge soaring birds, over the plain below the Embassy where we ride.

At eight o'clock seven or eight 'refugees' who were camping in the compound came in to have supper with us, two university teachers, a woman social worker, a business man from Kenya, and a chartered accountant and his wife. Others went to other houses. We sat up till eleven o'clock, the Military Attaché going out again (as the male staff had been doing in turns all day to report). He said that all was quiet except round the Palace and the Bodyguard headquarters which are near it, and which he could not approach. The university teachers had spent most of the day in their cellars, and a shell had fallen on the playing field. Yesterday we had told British subjects that they could come into the compound, and it was also broadcast from London that we would do this. But as the town's electricity supply had failed since the morning, many people did not know. Ronnie, the Consul, went round telling as many as he could. All night there was firing at intervals of half an hour to an hour. We slept through part of it and then at 6.30 a.m. some of the campers came up to our hall which had heavy stone walls, as bullets were coming into the compounds. Two hospital nurses who had been caught in the firing in town the day before were sleeping under the piano.

All the servants arrived as usual and we gave breakfast to fifteen people after lighting the fire in the hall to warm them. Just as we were having it, the Jarys, head teacher at the Palace school arrived. She was in tears, though relieved to get here, because for two days she had kept all the Emperor's grandchildren with her and refused to give them up to the Bodyguard soldiers. Then this morning some of the officers arrived and forced her to do so. The Palace grounds were full of tanks and ammunition, she said, and civilians all round were being evacuated in preparation for an attack by the Army expected at 10 a.m. So she and her husband decided to leave and drove up here in their car, and though very upset at giving up their responsibility they felt the children would be safer if taken away to wherever the rest of the family were. Only the Crown Prince was still somewhere in the Palace.

Thirty African Commonwealth students came in this morning too, so we had to prepare food. Some had brought their own, but we were quickly running out of bread. I told my cook to make as much as he could, and also stews which would do for any number for lunch. Our guest Sir Harry left with some field-glasses at 10 a.m. to climb the hill behind us and to see what he could of the Palace district.

But nothing developed of the concentrated attack on the Palace because the Bodyguard decided to 'parley' with the Army, and we just had some intermittent firing, and more and more patrolling in the air, including, eight jets over the compounds. The Fergussons, sitting outside their house in the morning, suddenly heard bullets whistling past from the direction of the road below, and had to go in. But the camp in the field was sheltered from the range of fire and grew and grew in proportions, until it was one hundred and twenty-five people for lunch, which they arranged for themselves once we – the Consul mainly – had provided large tents and all the camp equipment we possessed, plus water piped to a corner of the field. The thirty African students who had been brought up in a bus from the university had spent the night before on the floor and had had only biscuits for breakfast as all the food had run out. The proprietor of the Aurora Stores, a sort of 'village post office' shop, appeared with his wife, both British subjects. Food for the smaller children was looked after by Ann Joy from her house, while others had the camp kitchen, and the one girl African student, from Zanzibar, prepared the meals for her fellow Africans.

I sent down all our spare china and cooking pots, and large tin pans for heating water, and also collected more china and cutlery round the compound. Denis set off with the M.A. to try to get the two nurses back to their hospital where they knew they would be badly needed, but after going for half a mile down the road they were stopped by firing and eventually they got away late in the evening.

In two hotels in the town ninety women from different African countries, the U.S., England and the U.N. were housed for a conference this week. Ronnie Peel got through to them in a jeep and found that they had no casualties but were all terrified. Someone brought two Maltese nuns to the compound. Charles Wright, a Professor of Amharic, was wandering in the paddock, trying to stop someone's pet monkey from scratching his car; it would jump on the bonnet and look at itself in the windscreen, and he dislodged it, finally by turning on the wipers. Later the head of the camp brought him up to stay with us as he had no blankets, was rather delicate, and would have had to sleep with four others in the tent. He said his household had all left him to hide when they heard of the projected Palace attack, so he had put his bed in his car and come up here.

In the evening about fifty people left to go home again, including the university teachers and some of our own staff, worried about their property. The firing died down after sunset and no more planes came over, so that all seemed calm. But we heard that there had been about one thousand casualties, and that the Tsahai hospital, where there were British staff, was in urgent need of help. Several Europeans had been killed in the street, a French boy and a German.

The next morning I went down with Diana Peel, Harry Luke, and one of our servants to the hospital. The town was not as badly destroyed as we had expected, but there were smashed cars and taxis and many broken windows. There were bullet holes in the Ministry of Defence, and the walls and gates of the Palace were broken in many places. People were in the streets and a very few shops open. The most gruesome sight was the body of one of the instigators of the revolt, hanging from a rough gallows in the square by St. George's Church.

At the hospital the matron was exhausted, she said there was nothing in particular for women to do because they had no bandages to wash or roll, they were terribly short of dressings. Their one general surgeon had been operating up till two and three in the morning. What they needed most were stretcher-bearers, so we said we would get relays of the African students from our camp, and also blood-donors from the British community, as they could take twenty at a time. We visited some of the wards, where the wounded soldiers were lying on beds and on the floor, most of them completely silent. Some had arms and legs already amputated and bandaged, but nearly all were taking a little food, without meat as it is a fast day. The matron said that many had been brought in dead, the ambulance service is very poor, and the distances in the town are great; many soldiers had remained untended in their barracks.

We went back for lunch and found that there was to be a meeting of Ambassadors in our house at 5 p.m. and that some of the 'emergent African Women', stranded in the hotels, were being brought up for tea. Five appeared, in our car, two Nigerians in spectacular costume, a Colonial Office representative from England, and Miss Tomlinson, a seventy-nine year old welfare worker, full of spirit. Also a Girl Guide called Dame Whately, who had lined up all the delegates and led them from the conference hall back to their hotels through the firing, and had a bullet in her wide skirt. They said that the hotels had treated them with great friendliness, they ate in the kitchens, by candle-light at night. There had been a lot of shelling of the Jubilee Palace nearby, held by the Bodyguard for two days and nights. They had been rationed to one bottle of water a day.

During that Ambassadors' meeting the Emperor came back, with his grandson Alexander. They went to the Jubilee Palace, now evacuated. Firing became less and less, but the Army were winkling out the Bodyguard from all over the town and there were likely to be bursts anywhere where they were found to be hidden. An Englishman who drove into the compound in the afternoon said that some of the Bodyguard had been fighting in the street, and when one of them ran out of ammunition a crowd of people seized him and beat him to death. One of the officers, well known to people in our embassy, was let into the compound by the guards at the gate, though they had been told to refuse any Ethiopians. He went to the house of the accountant, Bebbington, but when Denis and the M.A. heard of it they said he must leave, because if the Army broke in to find him we could risk the lives of the staff, with the children running about, etc. So they gave him a stiff whisky, and with Mrs Bebbington and others in tears he was told to drive his car behind our M.A.'s to the nearest police station to give himself up. But in a large car he was very conspicuous; the M.A. lost touch, and we never knew what happened to him.

Yesterday afternoon, when the Bodyguard knew they had lost the battle, they shot most of the Ministers of the Cabinet whom they were holding in the Palace, including Blattadawit, a very well-known figure in the M.F.A. and a character of whom we were fond. He was like an old monkey, and used to joke about it. Ten days ago he was dining with us, as was Ande Mihail, the Vice-Minister of Information (and also, in fact, the handsome leader of the Bodyguard, Mengistu – hanged a week later in the market place, the greatest dishonour – who told me that his men rather resented the amount of money spent on food for their mascot, a lion). Makonnen Deneke, a soldier on the Emperor's staff, was only wounded when the others were shot, but lost both his legs.

The town today, Sunday, is recovering, and shops are said to be open, so that we can stop baking bread, and hope that tomorrow we can buy fruit, vegetables and milk again. We have not run short so far, owing to using stores from the Embassy shop, but would have in two day's time. The M.A. who has been staying with us is going home, and some journalists who were on the Emperor's plane from Khartoum to Asmara, and managed to find another plane from there, will be coming up to lunch.

Our servants all through have been very calm and helpful, especially Abdulla who is quicker than any of them to sum

Berhanu, our driver, and two Galla beauties

Christmas party for Embassy children, 1960

up a situation. They have raced about and at the same time not been excited. But when they heard of the Ministers being shot, all of whom they knew from their visits here, their eyes filled with tears, especially for old 'Blatta'. The Emperor we feel must be overwhelmed by all this chaos, many old friends dead and the Bodyguard, his 'children' as one of the servants said, the privileged and most spectacular part of his army with their lion-mane helmets and epaulettes, having revolted against him. Old Stephen Wright said that they had been too spoilt, and wanted more and more. What their exact connection was with all the university students and younger civil servants who demonstrated with them and seemed overjoyed at the prospect of a change of government, we do not know. There will have to be a new government, as the old are dead.

Chapter Fourteen

A Trip to the Yemen, April 1962

Before the death of the last Imam, we had the rare privilege of receiving from him a permit to visit the Yemen, while we were still in Ethiopia. There had recently been a shooting incident involving our Chargé d'Affaires to the Yemen, and their Ambassador in Addis Ababa was keen to make amends. We were going to Aden for a few days holiday, and when the military authorities there heard of our project they arranged an escort to the frontier for us, partly for our safety and partly as an exercise for the soldiers. We were to be met at the border by the Legation landrover from Taiz.

We set off soon after 8 a.m. in separate jeeps, part of a cavalcade which was headed by 'walkie-talkie' vehicles, and in the middle were two truckloads of soldiers in the charge of two British officers. The heat was very oppressive, and having been perpetually thirsty in Aden and drunk a lot of acrid water there, I felt sick and faint and could hardly keep myself from falling out of the jeep, which had no doors, as we bumped along the very rough track. We made several stops on the way, during the three hour drive, stretching our legs by the road side and drinking more water and lemon juice, while the soldiers, having leapt from the lorries, would deploy themselves around us.

After going three-quarters of the way through dry and stony

desert, the road began to curve among rocks and climb towards the hills of the Yemen. We reached the little village at the frontier where the landrover from the Legation was waiting, and left our convoy to rest a short time before returning. We ourselves set off at once and the more comfortable vehicle and cooler air as we climbed made me recover my balance. The road wound continuously, but as it went through a series of small hamlets it was not monotonous; there was a high mountain range ahead, and more and greener vegetation appeared.

Our driver had plenty to tell us about Legation life, and the people he had worked for, how often he had travelled this road, and where his passengers liked to have their lunch. There was a piece of shade under a tree in a dry river bed which was the most popular spot, and we eventually reached it and sat down to enjoy the food and wine sent by our future host, the Chargé d'Affaires, and to rest for a short time on the little patch of wiry, grey-green grass cropped short by sheep and goats.

It seemed long, as a strange road usually does, but after two or more hours we were up in the hills and expecting to see Taiz round every corner. We passed more and more people in Yemeni dress, returning from market in single file and carrying a great assortment of wares. The women wore black, with high necks and heavy embroidery down the front, over trousers cut in Chinese style, tight at the ankle. The men wore white Arab dress, belted and with daggers and often rifles as well.

When we reached the town it was nearly dark, but we entered a lighted courtyard almost immediately, through a wide arch spanning the road, and were told that this was part of the Imam's palace. We noticed that several men standing about had chains on the ankles, with heavy links about a foot long. These were criminals, frequently to be seen in the streets. The Chargé d'Affaires told us later that the Manager of the air-port, who had been held responsible for a recent air crash, had been put in chains for a time and had clanked about in them in his office.

After this long day in the sun, and the dust on the road which billowed back over us at every corner, we were glad to see the Legation coat-of-arms on a high mud wall, and to find inside a neat square house and sandy green with a gazelle in a cage in the corner. The ground floor consisted of an entrance hall which was a small guard room with two iron bedsteads and a rough table for the guards, heavily armed and quite frightening to see in the dim light, . . . and an office and kitchen. A stone stairway led up to a flat above and on up to the roof. Inside the heavy wooden door to the flat was a cool, attractive room, with bedrooms and small study leading out of it, and there our host made us very comfortable with refreshing drinks and the suggestion of a bath and a rest before dinner. He told us how his predecessor had been nearly murdered by a madman in this flat, but his wife had managed to reach the telephone below before the murderer had cut the wires, and help had come from another Legation, while the Imam had had the victim flown in his private 'plane to Aden, badly stabbed.

The story seemed unreal as we sat in the very English atmosphere of the sitting-room, with cretonnes and china and books, Maple's coffee tables and lamps familiar from other Embassies. But the sight of the guards below made one realise how quickly things can change.

The Italian Minister and his wife came to dinner, together with some visitors staying with them, and as he was one of the greatest authorities on the Yemen, the conversation was absorbing. He had also been, during the war, the person with the highest price put on his head by us, for his activities in the region. He now breeds horses, which he rides without bits, and he offered one to Denis to ride the next day.

We went to sleep with the sounds of the town round us . . . dogs barking, the guards shuffling and muttering, then the muezzin at sunrise . . . but no traffic in the streets, and no light beside the moon.

In the morning I sat on the roof while Denis went for his ride, and later went with him and the 'Chargé' to have coffee with the Italians. We walked back through the bazaar, drove in the afternoon to see a modern house which was to be our new Legation, near a large school where the Imam's sons were being educated . . . then went to the airport to wait for a small Yugoslav 'plane which would take us back to the hot, cosmopolitan atmosphere of Aden.

In 1963 Denis was sent as Ambassador to Tehran. Iran.

Chapter Fifteen

Two Houses 1963–71

In Tehran, six months of the year were cool or very cold, and six were hot, so that social events were held indoors from November until April, and outdoors for the rest of the time. It had been the custom for all rich Persian families to own two houses, one in the town and one in the foothills of the Elburz mountains, eight miles to the north, in what had previously been separate villages. Several foreign Embassies had two compounds and two Residences also, the Germans, the British, the Italians, Turks and Russians, while the Shah himself had five Palaces, two, gracefully ornate, belonging to his famous predecessor, Nasr-ud-din Shah, two of his father's and one of his own. At Saad-Abad, or 'Cool Place', round his father's summer Palace was a collection of houses for members of the Royal Family, set in a large Park which was surrounded by a high wall with gates always manned by sentries, and a river running through it which made it the coolest spot in summer.

By 1960 most Persian families with two houses had sold those in the town and lived entirely in their summer quarters, with oil heating in winter. The Shah also, for reasons of security, gave up his town Palace and made the old summer Palace of Nasr-ud-din Shah into his office. Only the foreign Ambassadors continued their twice-yearly migration, while all those countries who had established relations with Persia more recently than the Great Powers, chose houses for themselves in the cooler, higher suburbs.

131

Spectacular receptions were given in the various Palaces on the occasion of the visits of foreign Heads of State. The large rooms of the older Palaces had walls entirely composed of tiny mirrors, reflecting the dresses and jewels of the women and the uniforms of the men; also the lights of huge candelabras. Persian carpets covered the floors from wall to wall, having been woven to fit each room exactly. In summer, tables and carpets were transported to the gardens and lit by standing candelabras, the candles protected by glass shades. The nights were so warm that while men had white jackets the women could wear the thinnest of dresses. After the dinners there were displays of fireworks, and during the visit of King of Saudi Arabia, a fir tree caught fire, near the Palace balcony, and blazed dangerously near to the Arabs' flowing robes, while the Persian ladies shrieked and ran indoors; there were no Arab ladies present.

Our own reception rooms in the Tehran Residence dated from 1870. Two large rooms, with a hall between them, had ceilings of intricate plasterwork and high up round the walls medallions with the letter 'V' and shamrocks, roses and thistles. Between them were small, round, stained-glass windows, lit from the outside, and above the main windows which were pointed like those of a nineteenth century English church and fortunately covered by pale rose curtains at night. The walls were white and gold, and the floor of the large drawing room covered by a valuable Tabriz carpet, bought in England and admired by English and Persians alike. The small sitting room had been the Ambassador's study, until a new and separate office block had been built. It contained a large painting of Fath Ali Shah. This little room, entirely cube-shaped, and with a small chandelier to match the two large ones in the drawing room, opened into the larger room and from it, when the doors were opened in to the hall also, was an elegant vista leading to the portrait of Queen Victoria as a young Queen which hung at the very end of the big dining room and beneath which stood a silver vase full of flowers. We hung this picture in what seemed the most prominent and suitable position, as it was

ATO, our Dachshund, on the Shah's Coronation day

The British Embassy's Summer Camp in the Lar Valley near Tehran

previously on the side wall facing the windows and only visible inside the room. In its place went the portrait of the present Queen, whose photograph also stood on the grand piano in the drawing room.

Gertrude Bell, a visitor in 1892, wrote, 'We arrived . . . in the Garden of Eden with a very comfortable house built in the middle of it.' Arriving ourselves in 1963 we were just in time to see the wing in which she stayed being destroyed; the 'three windows opening onto . . . the tops of trees' were there long enough for us to photograph them, the trees now as tall again as the house itself. Lord Curzon, on a journey through Teheran, had noted that they were planted in 1870.

In place of the old private sitting-room of the Ambassador a new one was built with three walls entirely of glass. In winter, by a blazing fire, we looked out on the snow-covered lawn with the tall trees draped in white. The sun shone, and a dachshund raced happily through the snow. The ginger cat from a neighbouring house made a bright spot of colour, and was the object of the dachshund's flight. It was a cosy and peaceful scene, but not for very long. From a record kept over one year we had as many as seventy house-guests, who stayed a total of two hundred and forty nights with us; we had eight hundred people to lunch, one thousand eight hundred for 'cocktails' and nine hundred and twenty-five for dinner. Of these, only ten per cent of the house-guests were personal friends, whose visits we arranged at times when we could be free to entertain them. The rest were 'official', and as the 'planes from England or the Far East arrived mostly during the night, and members of the office staff would bring them from the airport, we did not see our guests until morning, when we would meet and introduce ourselves at the foot of the stairs or find them waiting for us in the sitting-room. Most of these guests had their own work to do. The servants' English vocabulary stretched to 'Breakfast, what time?' . . . 'Lunch?' . . . 'Dinner?' in order to find out when they would be with us for meals.

A picturesque occasion every spring was the 'Wisteria Party', given to celebrate the blooming of these plants which covered the long terrace on the garden side of the big reception rooms, their heavy-scented flowers hanging like bunches of pale grapes. The invitations were usually sent out as soon as the buds appeared, as the gardeners said they would flower two weeks later; if held too late, the terrace would be a carpet of petals. Persians in Teheran looked forward to this party, one of the first to be held out of doors. The large drawing room and dining room were cleared of furniture in case of cold weather, but guests preferred to wander outside, down the stone steps, and enjoy the early scents of spring. Although the compound was surrounded by busy shopping streets, and one or two tall buildings now over-looked it, the high walls, trees and shrubs made it still secluded. Bright blue parakeets nested in the trees, and a white bird, a squacco heron, settled for a week or so in a willow by the pool on its way south. Also the crystal hoopoe. In May the frogs began their nightly chorus, and even drowned some announcements made by loud speakers at the Queen's Birthday Party. After this last event came the move to the summer compound six miles away and once a day's journey for the Minister, when he, his family and staff would ride, and the servants walk with trays carrying the silver on their heads, while mules carried furniture; and now a short run in a car, a two-ton lorry carrying trunks, ornaments, china, glass and linen, while a second set of furniture had now been provided and remained there.

The Gulhak house had spacious rooms, but few. The central sitting-room entered from the front doorsteps, led through to a large balcony. Here we breakfasted, and spent most of the day as it was carpeted and arranged with comfortable sofas, chairs and small tables. The white ballustrades were lined with potted plants, and the steps leading to the garden, with oleanders and jasmine. At the bottom of the steps was a pool lined with blue tiles, and surrounded by a stone path; beyond it a lawn, and more tall plane trees. Woodpeckers and kestrels, and sometimes golden orioles flew about, and we heard the clear, monotonous sound of the skops owl at night.

The British Embassy Residence, Gulhak

The Balcony

As we breakfasted, wild cats would lurk among the plants, until the dog chased them onto the lawn, where he also kept watch for the large crows which would steal his food, walking along boldly with their rolling gait until he came very near. He enjoyed the freedom of this compound and would go long walks on his own, sometimes to visit a friend of the same breed in the house of the Air Attaché, where he would appear at an early hour in the family bedroom. When the days grew hotter, he slept indoors in the late morning, until the sound of the horn of the Rolls Royce at the main gate woke him, though we could not hear it, much less distinguish it from the horns of other cars; and he was on the front steps to welcome his master back from the office.

The large compound contained twelve other houses and a block of flats, as well as two tennis courts, a large octagonal swimming-pool and a school. Near our house was stabling for five horses, and a small exercise ground for them. The compound had formerly been planted with vines, fruit trees and vegetables as well as flowers, and there were still traces of the vines on an old pergola, and in terraces, but the old fruit trees no longer bore fruit and planes, oaks, silver birches, hawthorns and hazel now predominated. There was an avenue of purple lilacs, and in June a yellow rose, named Rosa Lutca, flowered in the same avenue. Between many of the houses there was wasteland with thick undergrowth, paths and streams of water running through it, so that one could go for a leisurely afternoon walk lasting nearly an hour, watching a game of tennis on the way.

Entertaining here was simpler. The dining room was large enough only for six or eight guests, and for more we had a large, embroidered tent set up on the lawn. For evening parties it was lit with lanterns and with candles, and coffee was served round the pool, where small lamps such as were carried by the Wise and Foolish Virgins stood on the low parapet and reflected in the water. We were provided with 'deck' chairs of every size and shape, some of which presented problems for the oldest of the servants, Sheikh Ali, when he tried to set them up. He would talk to himself and to them, while a younger servant stood by laughing. Most of the servants lived in quarters inside the compound, or in the village of Gulhak itself, so that life was easier for them in the summer months, with no bus journeys to and from Tehran, and a siesta each afternoon when work was slack. With only one spare-room, the other being occupied by my secretary, Jane, or later, Teresa, we could not accommodate many house-guests. When Jane once offered to sleep in a tent to make room for an extra guest, we set up one of the small Indian tents from the Embassy store, used for camping. It was of beautifully dyed and embroidered cotton, with a scalloped frill round the top and a small window with knotted string 'panes'. She went to bed happily, with a divan, carpets and cushions, but unfortunately during the whole night cats chased each other through the tent in all directions. Normally, as traffic, noise and dust accumulated in the centre of Tehran, Gulhak was a welcome refuge, cool and quiet. We were once dining with some Persian and American friends when the moving news came through that the first astronauts were on the moon. Returning, I took the dog out for his usual walk, and as he chased frogs in the brick culverts under the paths, and followed rustling sounds in the undergrowth, I looked up at the moon with the incredulity we all felt.

Life in Tehran became more and more social, for those in official positions as well as those just enjoying themselves, and a retreat like the pretty, elegant house and cool garden at Gulhak was more and more appreciated. We also travelled as much as possible to the other parts of the country, which were not changing so rapidly. For the first few years of our stay it was still possible to ride from the compound through narrow lanes into open country, where four or five of us could gallop in the desert, but plots of land were gradually fenced in, buildings appeared, and bull-dozers frightened the horses. Finally, the stables were closed, and Denis and I rode only, by invitation, from the Royal stables, where with Persian friends and a groom we could follow a small valley, full of wild flowers in the spring, and rounding a hill would see a herd of mouflon grazing.

When it became too cool in autumn to entertain outside we had to leave Gulhak, as rains came which would spoil the tent. Once more the big room of the larger house in town had to be opened, and house-guests would arrive. It was cosy at night to see the brightly lit streets outside, as winter approached and stalls selling roast chestnuts and hot beetroots appeared and finally, for the foreigners, rows and rows of Christmas trees, stacked outside the walls of the British, Embassy from long custom.

Saint Andrews Night in Tehran

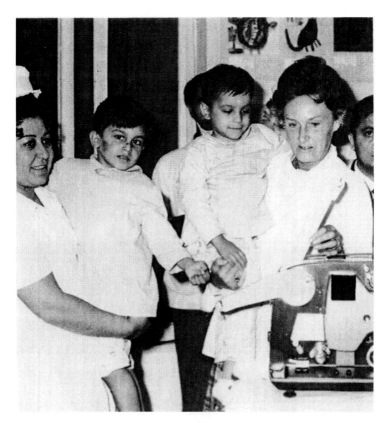

Giving a projector to an orphanage in Tehran

Chapter Sixteen

Trip to Afghanistan September–October 1967

We left Meshed at 7.30 a.m. The old Consulate now used by the British Council was as lovely as ever; the spacious ramshackle house with its colonnade of white pillars round three sides, dark hall, heavy stone staircase and, above, creaking wood floors, but large, low rooms, with wide windowsills, and English cretonnes on comfortable sofas and chairs. In our bathroom there was an old copper water-heater, encased in a rough wooden screen. On our last visit this had been roaring and crackling to heat the bath-water, but this time it was stone cold. However, the Pakistani servant said that if we ran the tap long enough, hot water would come from a new system of pipes, and it eventually did, but the old boiler will probably remain and become a curiosity.

Outside in the compound the other staff houses, also dating from the last century, had been pulled down, as not having been used since the Consulate was closed, they had fallen into ruin. But roses and dahlias were in full bloom in the big garden, and the hedges were neatly clipped. Round the old swimming pool, with its flights of stone steps leading down to one level and then to a lower one, the huge, shady willow trees were flourishing. It is a sad decaying place in many ways, and very silent now, but even so, much better than a modern hotel. It is quiet even though on the main street, because of the high walls, and solid gate-house.

We set off with Lev Tamp in our landrover, while the Tonkins followed in their 'dormobile', and they were followed by the three Germans in the party. Lev, who is a Persian subject but originally came from Russia, had spent his time in Meshed with some old Russian friends, and they had given him a cigar bought forty-two years ago in Berlin! Lev smoked this as we went along, and said that it was surprisingly good.

Travelling with the German Military Attaché in our party we were entertained by the army posts near the Afghan frontier with tea and melons. Once inside Afghanistan we got quickly to Herat on an American-made road, and stayed in a Russian-made hotel, comfortable and of startling modern design, the walls between the rooms on the ground floor were openwork in black zig-zags. We slept well although some had bugs in their beds; the food was very good at dinner and there were fresh eggs for breakfast.

We started the first part of the journey to Kabul by the northern, more difficult route. None of the road was asphalted after Herat, and luckily the Tonkins discovered a broken spring in time and could get it repaired immediately for less than one pound, and with a wait of only a few hours. So we went off eventually, in caravan, taking it in turns to be in the lead. Our first night was spent in camp, in a dry river-bed, but with a small irrigation canal running nearby which had enough clean water in it to at least wash and wash-up in. We had a good supper of ravioli and bully beef, after soup, and then melon. By 8.30 we were in bed, in bright moonlight, after one or two local people had called in on us, some of them with maladies to be cured as they had heard that Richard was a doctor. One with a sore eye sat at our camp table for a while, with two small boys crouching on their heels nearby, staring with friendly round eyes. They tried some fudge and liked it.

During the night we woke to hear footsteps past the tents, and later a voice talking to Nosrat, our driver. It turned out to be the police, who, having been told from Herat that we were coming, had driven from the nearest village ahead, to find us. In the morning there they were, five of them, in ragged uniforms, and we gave them tea. They had no rifles. As Lev said, "Very interesting, police has no arms, . . . but tribesmen, all is armed." After some pushing they got their jeep to go off ahead of us to their village, where we were treated to a tasty second breakfast of hot milk and a sort of pancake, in the town hall of Ghormach, or rather in its garden, sitting in a tent especially erected in our honour, full of brightly coloured cushions and set among zinnias, petunias and fruit trees. Afterwards we visited the market place, as it was market day for animals, people took very little notice of us as we were led round by our host at breakfast, the head-man of the village.

From then on to Maimana, where there was a comfortable hotel, and to Akcha, Mazar-i-sharif and Gunduz, where there were government rest-houses run by simple, pleasant people and incredibly cheap. Dinner, bed and breakfast, and a rudimentary bathroom with both shower and bath, cost 11/- per head. The towns were all quiet after about 9 p.m. when the cinema sound-track, broadcast outside, stopped, the markets had closed at 7 p.m. and only dogs barked, but as the beds were always comfortable and we were tired from the road, we did not stay long awake.

From Qala-i-nou to Maimana was a long dusty drive through a valley, only 1,000 ft. up, so still hot in September. And after Maimana we were in open steppe country, mile after mile of winding track over small buff-coloured rises, and sometimes long stretches of perfectly flat and hard turf, with nothing in sight in any direction, though in spring there would be flowers and good grazing, but no water for flocks. We had a guide, in a Russian jeep, which was filled with people and served as a bus, and twice we had to tow it out of deep sand patches, as its four wheel drive was broken. This journey took us only three hours, compared to one of nine or more on a rutted road, and was well worth-while also for the feeling of space, so like Russian steppe country that at any moment it would not have been a surprise to see some Cossacks riding through the dust-haze.

When we reached Sheberghan, the town on the other side, we lunched on 'shish-kebab' and melon, washed briefly and went on to Akcha, where we had been told there was a good market for saddles, horse-trappings etc. All round here, horses were the main means of transport, and were fat and well-cared for, gaily decorated, too, in the droshkys in the towns. The only motor traffic was jeeps, lorries, and a few buses, but in a day we would only pass three or four of any of these. The exception was the road to Akcha, pitted with holes filled with fine dust, and travelling in the evening we met bus-loads of workers, our landrover completely disappearing in billowing dust-clouds as we passed them, luckily in daylight. The road had once been paved, as Lev said, but then, left to deteriorate, was worse than no road at all. "For miles and miles they brought these stones, and for what? The road is worse than the desert . . .' We continually made detours into the desert on either side, often passing elegant horsemen trotting or cantering easily along, compared to our ungainly progress. They were always in costume, long striped coats, and with the end of their turbans hanging down over one shoulder like a heavy tress of hair.

From time to time dogs rushed at us, guarding their flocks. "What faithful animals are these," said Lev, "what courage. They see a big animal like this landrover . . . any other animal would run away." The dogs came from tribal settlements, sometimes permanent, the first stage after leaving their tents. As Lev said, that was how the ownership of the land came about. "Slowly, slowly, they build a house, they grow vegetables. Then, in Iran, Turcoman was having his vegetable garden, Reza Shah comes along. Officials say, where are your papers. Of course they had none, they never took the land from anyone." Lev would like to spend nine months of the year in the wilds like this, living among the Turcomans, and three months in Europe. I wonder if he would not find the contrast too great.

In Gunduz, which has an asphalt road to Kabul, only six hours away, the hotel was a stage further in decoration and amenities than the others we had stayed in (though all had had thick, richly coloured Afghan carpets on the floor, deep red-purple, stretching from wall to wall). Here metal chairs with plastic leather seats replaced the wooden ones, there was a second storey to the building, and heavy wrought-iron banisters. The ceilings were decorated with plaster cubes and circles and flowers. There was also a refrigerator, for iced water which we had not seen since Herat. The heat in the steppe country made one perpetually thirsty, at this time of year, and we had tried to make our drinking water from Meshed last out, by varying it with water melons which were the local form of thirst-quencher for travellers, bought as they went along. But in Gunduz fresh lemon juice was produced and we could drink our fill. The tea which is produced everywhere, also helps in spite of the heat, usually the green Chinese type.

After eight days travelling, from 7.30 a.m. till 4 or 5 p.m. every day, we reached our furthest point east, and the main object of the trip, a remote valley with a rushing trout river, reserved for the King or for persons with his permission to fish. The fish are perhaps not so much the main object of the permits as the proximity of the Russian frontier, but it is also part of the Royal game reserve and hunting grounds. The grassy verge of the river is carefully tended by an old man, who waters several small trees there every day, planted round a kind of natural dais, presumably for the King's tent. Here we stayed in a cool breeze and warm sun, washing our clothes in the river and then settling down to reading, writing or fishing. We were guarded by the old man. He had a long beard, a long cotton gown and white turban and appeared to be the Royal gardener. His coat, like a ragged dressing-gown with lumps of cotton padding showing in places, had long sleeves which he used for banging the dust off the small trees. Occasionally he talked to Nosrat our driver and once he brought us some pears but refused any payment.

The second day was misty, and very like Scotland. It grew very cold and we spent the evening in the Germans' tent, more solid and larger than ours, drinking whisky and brandy to warm ourselves. Lev went off on a bus to a tea-house further up the river, where he slept the night and enjoyed all the questioning of the local inhabitants. They lent him some bedding. 'I ask them,' he said, 'how many lions and tigers you have in these blankets to bite me?'

In Kabul we stayed at the Embassy, the imposing white building with arches in front and at the back, flat lawns and flower borders leading down to a rose garden, a pergola covered with a vine, and in the distance blue hills. There were no sounds from the town, only voices from the tennis court and swimming pool. The house is long, three storeys in the centre and two at the sides, with a central baronial-style hall hung with swords and trophies, on dark panelling. A ballroom opens out of it on the garden side, and on the right and left are dining-room and sitting-room, the latter painted white by a recent Ambassadress, with high white mantelpieces and casement curtains. The bedrooms too are white, with Wilton carpets, chintzes, and white-tiled bathrooms, so home-like and far removed from the semi-modern town outside the gates, and from the luxury hotel now being built, and even more so from old Kabul to the south, dirty and smelly, as Lev says, 'You can't imagine how the people live.'

The pack mules

Chapter Seventeen

A Ride in Mazanderan, August 1969

We set off from Teheran at 9.15 a.m., having waited for our travelling companion Lev Tamp, who had been summoned to the Ministry of War about some cavalry horses. He said he had been asked to go there at 7 a.m. and then, as he waited impatiently, they kept bringing him water-melon to eat, and he could neither find anyone to speak to, nor leave.

However we had time in hand and once started in the landrover we went by the old road to the Caspian, through Firouzkuh. As we ran alongside the railway for some time, Lev told us stories of when it was built, and he himself was working on it, after coming to Iran as a young refugee from the Russian Revolution. He knows the country well since that time, and has many Iranian friends in the small towns and villages. One of these was a local landlord and squire of his village, named Mr Espabodi, who was to take us on this ride. We turned off the rain road at Pul-i-Sefid, and drove for a couple of hours through rolling country, alternately thickly forested or descending to rice paddies in low valleys, until we reached a village called Gortcheh. Here our host-to-be lived in a long white house with a grey timber roof, beautifully carved and painted under the eaves, and on the ceilings of the main rooms with gay designs of flowers and birds, like churches in the West Country of England. Lev had been here the year

147

before, on a hunting trip, and had persuaded us to repeat it with him. From a balcony, which overhung the main street, we looked across the rice paddies to wooded hills, and beyond them to a high rocky ridge, over and behind which we were to go, though it was hard to believe that horses would take us all that way and back in eight days. Apart from the rice, the country-side and the villages with their timber roofs and carved balconies looked just like Switzerland, especially as sleek black-and-white cows were grazing by the road side. We were at 900 feet only above sea level, and the temperature was mild and damp. We had a neat bedroom with wooden beds covered by quilts stuffed with wool. The quilts had sheets sewn on one side of them but the upper side was made of embroidered cloth from Kerman, now rare but once used for elaborate coats of the rich in Persia. There was also a piece on the wall and on the table, in vivid red with darker red pattern. In an adjoining room was a small table holding a basin and ewer, and next to it a Moslem lavatory. For the next eight days we were to live like this, washing only in running water, usually a servant would pour the water over one's hands, or we would do it for each other, as to wash in still water is not considered clean by Moslems. In houses where there was a balcony this can be done only with the ewer, and the water splashes down into the garden or street below, but altogether very little washing was done until the fourth day, when we were treated to a complete bath, or *hammam*, in the mountain village where Mr Espabodi's family spent the summer. We were also to see no chairs, tables or beds for the next four days.

Tonight we sat on tubular aluminium chairs said to be made in England, on the balcony, and Mr Espabodi told stories of his post-war adventures with brigands in this area, when he was given arms by the Persian Government to restore 'law and order', (which meant usually his own law and that of his friends), against pro-Russian Persians who were getting support while Russian forces were still in occupation. We drank some whisky which we had brought with us, and ate pistachios. Mr Espabodi was not averse to a little whisky at times, though Lev said he was drinking less now as he was sixty-eight and wanted to go to heaven. He said his prayers several times a day also. As we sat it grew dark, and with no electricity we enjoyed the clear white light of pressure lamps, and listened to sounds in the village, cows lowing, riders trotting or cantering by beneath us.

We were served a large dinner, mostly food of which we were to eat a great deal each day, hungry from our exertions, and which was extremely good; a chicken soup with lemon and egg yolk and chopped liver, then a lamb or chicken kebab, then rice done in different ways with a stew of egg plant to go with it, as well as various sauces, pickles and yoghurt. A great delicacy, which appeared in the peasants' houses we stayed in later, was a boiled sheep's head on a plate, which the host took, and with a spoon scooped out the brain, cut out the tongue, and passed them round to everyone. We usually finished with some Iranian tinned fruit, a concession to foreigners probably, and because fresh fruit was not available in the mountains.

The next day, after a breakfast on the balcony of cheese, butter, cream, eggs, honey and bread, Nescafé or tea, we mounted horses brought over by Mr Espabodi's son-in-law, and rode for only half-an-hour to a river, where Denis and Lev fished very successfully for trout, and I sat on the bank reading while one of our many attendants brought me some blackberries in a fig leaf. This day was to be an easy one, but we had a large meal, including the trout, at the home of Ahmad Khan, the son-in-law, before returning to Ghortcheh. Ahmad Khan married one of Mr Espabodi's children when she was only fourteen, and they already had five children, all jolly and healthy with curly black hair like their parents. Their mother was now a capable young housewife of twenty-two or so, who was going to look after the house and farm while we were away. As she joined us for lunch and sat next to me shyly, her father asked her why she had not kissed him. She blushed, but did not do so until we moved on to the balcony at the end of the meal. Mr Espabodi has had two wives, the first one had died after having five children, but the one whom we were to meet later was the mother of nine more, and this was her eldest daughter. Several of the older ones were in America, and others, Lev said, preferred to wander about Lalazar (the Tottenham Court Road of Tehran) rather than work on their father's land, though this was where their money came from.

Ahmad Khan, along with other landlords, had had to give up a large part of his land during land reform. Some time later, in fact only a few months ago, the villagers attacked him, wanting his house and garden as well. He called in a gendarme to help him, but they beat him so badly that Ahmad Khan went off to see the brother of the Shah, with whom he had been on hunting expeditions. The Shah's brother appealed to the Governor of Mazanderan who sent seventy gendarmes in place of the severely injured one. These managed to restore order, but Ahmad Khan had to feed them all for several weeks. His own house was not ostentatious and he was obviously a very diligent person, making a tidy and prolific garden in the few years since he had married. He had a small bar displaying bottles of foreign wines and liqueurs, and his father-in-law complained that he was too fond of drinking vodka with his friends, but as he was a cheerful and jolly person this may have been his compensation for living in a place with absolutely no recreations except hunting and fishing. He was just in the process of putting electricity in his house, wires were hanging down from the centre of the ceilings in the rooms, and he was waiting for the dynamo; but there were no telephones to any of these villages off the main road, and we never met a policeman or soldier on the whole of our trip, unlike most parts of the country. Until two years ago it was a seven hour ride to Pul-i-Sefid on the main road, where Espabodi had an agent who received and sent letters for them and arranged motor transport between there and Tehran. Lev said that Ahmad Khan would do the ride in five and a half hours but 'almost killing' the horses.

Lev was delighted to be with his friends, and doing this trip again, on 'horzaback' as he called it. He said the villages reminded him of the one in which he lived with his parents before the Revolution, and which he thought he would inherit. He remembers being dressed in the national dress of that region of the Caucasus as a small boy, and says that if he could he would go back there and live just as simply today.

I sat on the balcony after lunch while the others fished again, and Mr Espabodi went to say his prayers, for which he put on a basque beret, and I could hear him intoning from the Koran in a room nearby. I tried to paint the view, of giant dahlias and climbing roses in the garden, and the rice fields and the forests beyond, until he joined me and began talking about Raphael. He was widely read and a good talker, though he made no allowance for us not being Persians, and we often had to bring Lev in to translate the long stories.

We drove back in a jeep in the evening to Mr Espabodi's house, from where we were to set off early the next morning, packing as few things as possible into saddle bags brought by Lev. Now, before the start of the journey, he supervised all the saddling of the horses and the loading of the mules. He had his own saddle and for Denis he brought another, Western style but made in Afghanistan, high at the back and front and very comfortable for the mountain riding, with a bright cloth over it. I had an English army saddle which he had given to Mr Espabodi for his wife to travel on up to their *Yayla*, as she had complained that they had no comfortable saddles. This one was comfortable but needed polishing, as the flaps were curled from dryness.

We were all assembled on the lawn in front of Mr Espabodi's house, with a great many servants standing round, when it began to rain. After a couple of hours it cleared enough for us to set off, riding through the low arch and out of the yard, through the village, a cavalcade of five horses and two mules. Mr Espabodi rode a thin white horse which he said was very strong, but with his check shirt, light linen suit, and panama hat he looked as nonchalant as Don Quixote, except for the revolver on his hip, and the horse very much like 'Rosinante'. Taking the lead he set the pace, and we moved along slowly, through meadows where cows grazed, and then began to climb through thick, damp beach woods. Mr Espabodi smoked as he went, and occasionally turned to shout directions to the servants or *tufangjis* (hunters), who accompanied us in the rear. We rode for several hours, climbing steeply over a shoulder of the mountain and then down as steeply to a river, where we had to walk as the horses slipped on the wet turf, though by now the sun was shining through the beech leaves and was very hot when we came out into the open. We continued for some time through low bushes on a mountain-side some way above the river, until we reached a village where lunch was prepared. All through our trip, someone went ahead to arrange for the meals and a night's rest, with friends of Mr Espabodi, and in each case a clean and tidy room was ready for us in a peasant's house, where we could eat and sleep, with often our saddles and baggage piled in a corner, but no furniture. Most houses were above ground level, as the lower part was used for animals and storage. It was delightful to be able to climb up to the balcony off which all the rooms lead, and sink on to the cotton quilts and bolsters which were provided, and laid on the carpet or felt rugs which stretched over the whole floor. First of all tea would be brought, and sugar bowls placed on the carpet beside us, then we would wash from the jug provided on the balcony, where we also left our shoes, and after a short rest, during which we nearly fell asleep, so comfortably stretched on the floor, the table cloth would be laid across the carpet and members of the family, male only, would bring in the dishes. Lev, Mr Espabodi and Ahmad Khan, and the head of the family, would come in for the meal, but rest in another room, where they could gossip over glasses of tea, and Lev would smoke his pipe. Everyone seemed in some awe of Mr Espabodi, and most of them always stood in his presence, but if they sat, it was in a kneeling position, with their hands palms downwards on their knees. Those who served were usually dressed in dark suits and open-necked shirts, and they would come in and out in their stockinged feet, taking great pains to offer things on the right side and to me first which would not normally be done with a woman, but Mr Espabodi gave grunts at intervals like a stage prompter, and at other times would call sharply "Serve the dinner!", "Bring water!", "Get the horses!"; his most frequent cry was for *Chai* (tea) which he drank more than twenty times a day, and would send a rider ahead, as Lev said 'to tell them to prepare immediately tea', and as the villages were often three or four hours distant from each other 'on horzaback', we also were glad of it.

The arrangement for meals made with the villagers saved us having to carry any food with us, but Mr Espabodi made one of the men carry what he called the 'filask', a thermos filled with tea, and after two hours riding it was very pleasant to sit under a tree, or down by a river, and have some of the strong brew, in the thermos lid. The Persians take a lump of sugar and suck the tea through it. We appreciated both the tea and the meals from the start. The riding and the fresh air gave us an appetite, but no-one forced us to eat more than we wanted. Lev did not like chicken, and Mr Espabodi always had his joke about this, asking someone to pass some to him, as it was always on the menu, but then to follow it up quickly with some liver kebab, or some stewed aubergines with yoghourt.

After lunch on the first day we had to ride on for another two and a half hours, and we only arrived at the final stopping-place after dark. For the last half mile the horses were feeling their way, which they knew well, along a river, and finally crossed it up to their chests in water, but on the further bank we could see someone with a lantern, who led us through the village. We reached a house built round a courtyard, already filled with people and with animals, and here ours were unsaddled and our sacks of clothes and bedding taken to a room furnished only with a carpet and some wall alcoves over which embroidered cotton cloths were hung. It had a fireplace, and carved wood shutters to the windows. None of the village houses had glass in their windows, but the shutters served also for protection from robbers. This house belonged to a famous ex-brigand named Baba Ali, now tall, thin and wrinkled. He had belonged to a famous brigand band when young, but he had lost his popularity when he betrayed one of the leaders. Later he joined the Government forces, as Mr Espabodi had, to fight communists after the war, and that had re-instated him with the local people, so that he now was one of the elders of this village.

In the morning we washed from a stream, which was piped into the yard and gushed out below the balcony. The yard was clear, except for our horses which had been brought out of the stables into one corner. Suddenly a woman of the family went over to a tiny door in the wall of the house, opened it and a stream of chickens came hurtling out, rushed to drink water where we were washing, and to eat the corn which was scattered for them.

We continued on our way, Mr Espabodi riding a mule as 'Rosinante' was tired from the day before, and was only carrying some saddle bags. Denis was on a handsome chestnut mare, Lev on a sturdy mountain pony, Ahmad Khan on a fine black gelding, and I on a strong, small horse which was more like a mule and in places where others had to dismount it carried me safely along, watching the ground as it went, and seldom stumbling. Behind us rode a servant, and the *tufangji* with the guns and fishing rods, while a young boy, about fourteen years old, walked nearly the whole way, except for crossing rivers, when he jumped up behind one of the men. He had to keep the mules from straying, and often carry the precious 'filask' of tea.

At first we ambled through lanes with hedges of blackberries and wild roses, then as the rice paddies along the river prevented us from taking a lower path, climbed high up into the forest again. After nearly an hour, when we had reached an old castle perched on a high bluff, Denis caught sight of an ibex on some rocks above a step precipice. Lev, Ahmad Khan and the hunters went after it, and Ahmad Khan shot it, only for it to fall down the precipice, so that it could not be brought up. He climbed right down and brought back a piece of its flesh to show he had killed it, but Denis regretted having pointed it out to them.

We had lunch in another village, again near the river, and then rode on for two hours down a wide valley, higher than the last so that rice was not grown there. It was roughly cultivated, but the people did not seem to be so prosperous as those who could grow rice and keep cows as well as sheep and goats. As we rode, we could see in the distance something which resembled a small pavilion, among tall trees, with two storeys and a balcony round it. Reaching the village near it, we found it was part of a large country house property, built more than one hundred years ago, but since fallen into decay. We came to big gates under an arch, and rode through a wide stone passage into the garden in front of the house. This consisted of the usual *biruni* (men's section) and the *anderuni* (women's) of old Persian houses, as well as a third large building across the street where we were to stay. All had been highly decorated with painting on wood and stucco work, and there were still faded medallions showing angel-like figures with garlands of flowers. There were innumerable rooms, all inhabited by many families of peasants, and some used as store rooms for hay which we could see through the broken shutters. Chickens ran in and out and many cats. We were given a small room on the upper floor, swept and carpeted, with carved windows and doors, at the top of a staircase of wood which might have been in an Elizabethan house in England. The windows still had coloured glass in the fanlights above them, and the walls had plaster carvings, white-washed. There were many empty rooms on the same floor, but downstairs there was a honeycomb of more rooms, poorly lit but full of people, some of whom were related to Mr Espabodi. They seemed rather dispirited, and the village as a whole gave an impression of poverty compared to the others we had seen. Although this may have been due to its position in the valley, and to its having less cultivable, it looked more as though the hangers-on of the old family were not able to turn their hand to other work when they needed to. A child was ill and Mr Espabodi gave instructions as to what to do for it, as the nearest doctor was four hours ride away. Certainly no-one had any idea of repairing the old house, or of the value of the carving and paintings, and the little pavilion on closer inspection had collapsed inside and was filled with hay.

There was a full moon over the garden, which lost its drabness at night and seemed like other Persian gardens, better preserved. We slept well in our room, though we put up our low canvas 'safari' beds to be more comfortable than lying on the floor.

The next day after nearly three hours riding we reached the *yayla* or summer resort where Mrs Espabodi and five of the children were staying. The path was extremely steep and rocky, with a precipice to one side, so that we walked most of the last part, the village with the old house showing as a patch of green far away and below. It was difficult to believe that everything modern that we found in the Espabodi's house here, household equipment, tables, chairs, carpets, doors, windows and gates, had been carried up by mules and donkeys, and the small children and old people managed that steep ride. To go directly back to the village of Ghortcheh took eight hours, instead of the two days we had taken to see more of the countryside.

The house was a low bungalow, with about six rooms, and a bath house in the garden. We were given a large room with two beds, a chair, a fireplace, and wide windowsills which served as tables. In a 'sitting room' next to it was a small table, four steel chairs and a good Persian carpet, while our bedroom and the other rooms had felt rugs, or *namads*, brown with attractively coloured designs and stamped on them. The chairs from the sitting room were sometimes brought for us to sit on for meals, as they were amused at our difficulty in sitting crosslegged round the table cloth, which sometimes reached almost to the wall and left very little space.

After lunch on the first day the bath water was heated and we could sluice ourselves with warm water, standing in a small stone room and baling it out of a stone tank, into which we were allowed to go when clean, as it had steps in it like a swimming pool.

Mrs Espabodi lent me some slippers to keep on in the house instead of taking on and off my own shoes every time. She was a good hostess, running things easily with the help of several small servant girls and a woman named *Nargess* (Narcissus), who wore the Mazanderani costume, bright red or green trousers and a short full skirt, with a white blouse and red head scarf, so much gayer than the Persian *chador* worn in Tehran.

After our bath we sat on the balcony and heard some shattering sounds as Lev and one of the young sons shot at a target on the hill opposite. Lev was going to set out at 4 a.m. on the next day on a hunting expedition with Ahmad Khan, but we were to spend the day resting and reading. Mr Espabodi went off to pray, then later appeared in a dark suit and with a tie, to receive callers from the village, but he sent Ahmad Khan out later to repay the calls.

The next day, apart from a walk to the source of the river, in a rocky gorge about a mile away, we stayed quietly in the house, left to ourselves to read or write, and to have another bath. The next morning we left early, saying many goodbyes, for the mountain tops and a higher valley, where the tribes from the other side of the range come up in summer, the 'Sangsari' from Semnan and Shahrud. The villagers from the *yayla*, which was called 'Hey Kuh', (many mountains) also take their flocks up there, but keep to their own encampments.

After climbing steadily for an hour, we reached a crest like the top of a pass from which we could see a long distance up a wide valley, not so far below us, dotted with the black tents of the 'Sangsari'. We rode down to the first group, which turned out to be the 'Hey Kuh', but then on to a much larger camp of 'Sangsari' about half an hour's distance from the other. Mr Espabodi then suggested that we should not stop but should ride to the northern ridge of the valley, not far away across grassy slopes, to see the view over Mazanderan. There was a cool breeze, and warm sun, as we rode along, and only the height would have stopped the horses cantering. When we reached the edge, there was a tremendous precipice below us, reaching down to the blue forests which stretched to the Caspian Sea, with faint strips of light green, the rice paddies in the valley we had come from. We went slowly back over the springy turf, passing flowers such as one would see on the Sussex Downs, camomile, daisies, coltsfoot, small foxgloves, scarlet pimpernel . . .

We had lunch with the 'Sangsari' in a large camp, where Lev joined us, having spent the night up in a higher range of mountains, at nearly 11,000 feet, where it was so bitterly cold that the tribes there were moving down to warmer pastures in ten days time. He found nothing to shoot, but had enjoyed himself, in spite of the cold. The goat hair tents are draped from pole to pole, looking like an impressionist picture of small groups of pine trees whose branches dip and interlace with one another. We sat in one of them, on a large raised platform, covered with carpets and with cushions round the sides. There were two other rooms, one for the women, and one as a kitchen and store. All round was a wall of clay about two feet high, to keep out the draught, and in the centre of the main room was a small well in which the fire could be made. Although the goathair looks thick from the outside, from inside it is much more transparent, and light rain began to come in as we sat there, but when the fire was lit the smoke seeping through the roof seemed to keep the rain out.

The lunch was one of the best we had, the 'Sangsari' being a very prosperous tribe with good flocks; the meat, cream, butter and yoghourt were all excellent. After a rest and a walk through the 'village', we went off to our quarters for the night, once again with the 'Hey Kuh' in another camp. Rather to our disappointment we were given a small hut, recently built and consisting of two rooms, to sleep in instead of a tent with the rest of our party. It rained more heavily, and all our baggage was brought in and stored in the entrance porch. We sat round the small room, on rugs and felts, the guns stacked in a corner, Mr Espabodi with his small suitcase in front of him, Ahmad Khan with his legs tucked under him like a plump Buddha. The whisky, or *chai Escotland* as Mr Espabodi called it, came out but was found to be empty. 'Unjeki (that one) finish' he said, and brought out the second. He was wearing his beret because of the cold. After a good supper, at which some of the men of 'Hey Kuh' joined us, the fire was lit and we sat in the smoke while Mr Espabodi reminisced about world history, from which we seemed particularly remote. By the time we went to sleep the fire had died to glowing embers.

We all had breakfast together, the Nescafé being brought out of the suitcase and drunk with hot sheep's milk. It was raining still, and cold. While Denis was shaving outside, wearing a thick pullover and windjacket, an old lady came in to light the fire again, glancing through the little window as she talked in case any man should come in, and she would have to flee, though tribes-women, and particularly older ones, are not so shy as village women. It was the same old lady who had led me to the camp lavatory the night before, with a hurricane lamp and a jug of water. On the way she bemoaned the fact that they were so far from the road and life was so hard. We passed a donkey in the dark and she said "There! There is *my* 'machine'!" (car). I gave her a tin of shortbread, as the tin was attractive and would be useful too. We rode off in the rain through the camp, its residents watching us, looking like a group of Highlanders in the old times, the men in homespun suits, and the women in bright skirts, jackets and head scarves.

We now rode along the high plateau for some time, before we came to a cleft in the northern edge of it, through which we were to descend the precipitous cliff and reach the forests again. Luckily the rain had stopped and the rocky path was not wet, as Lev who had been down it before said that it was nearly impossible if it was slippery with mud and loose stones. It was narrow and broken, passing between big boulders and twisting every ten yards. There were said to be one hundred and forty-five turns to the bottom. We scrambled down ahead of the cavalcade, looking only at our feet as to trip would mean a fall of many hundred feet, Mr Espabodi limping from arthritis, but sure-footed. At one or two places we met travellers coming up and the muleteers shouted to each-other to make room. The animals could easily fall to the bottom here, if they jostled their loads against others coming up. At last we reached wider paths and some scrub and long grass with mountain flowers. Mr Espabodi said that all the year round there were some flowers in bloom. Then there were beech trees and soft leafy paths, but still steep enough for us to have to walk to save the horses. At last we came to small open meadows, where cows were grazing, cows which themselves had recently been driven down here from the *yayla*. After another couple of hours, alternately in woods and clearings, we reached the first village, much resembling that of Mr Espabodi, a cluster of timber-roofed houses in a cleft in the meadows.

From a long way off we could see a reception committee of men waiting for us on the hillside, but did not realise until we reached them that they had a sheep ready to sacrifice in our honour. Suddenly I saw it lying in front of us, kicking, though the head was severed and the blood was all over the path. We were supposed to ride through this, but I did not know that was the custom, and as my horse shrank back, I asked the young boy with us to lead him to one side.

We arrived at a house in time for lunch and found a pleasant airy room prepared, leading off the usual balcony and with windows on three sides, giving a view over the village, and up to the mountain tops we had left that morning. In the afternoon I tried to paint this view, with a quaintly timbered house in the foreground and the lavatory, a little wooden hut at the end of a path through the garden, almost hidden in tall sunflowers. When I was led there by one of the peasant girls, she walked in front of me carrying a copper jug, and wearing pale green trousers, a white blouse and yellow head scarf, matching exactly the sunflowers which leant over us from each side.

We had our last dinner all together, and talked while Lev smoked his pipe; down in the lowlands the villagers had different problems to discuss.

Each night we had gone to bed at nine o'clock, and were up

by six or seven in the mornings. Leaving at seven again on the last day, we rode for some time along a grassy track, negotiable by landrover, one of which we met as part of a survey for a motor road in the future. Otherwise there were only a few riders and pedestrians, until we reached the rice paddies again and could see the villages of Ahmad Khan and Mr Espabodi across them, and met more people walking to their work. There were rain clouds coming up from the north and we realised how lucky we had been so far. We reached Ahmad Khan's house and found his wife waiting for us with lunch prepared, but there was no sign of our landrover and driver from Tehran, so after lunch we packed ourselves and all our baggage into Ahmad Khan's jeep and bumped our way over to Mr Espabodi's house, where we found the landrover had just arrived. The road was already difficult owing to light rain, so we left immediately, though regretfully, after our pleasurable holiday, set to the pace of riding and to village life, but anxious about the long drive ahead in the rain and partly in the dark.

We were only just in time, Nosrat our driver, manoeuvering the mud skilfully with the help of the four wheel drive, but at one point, going down a hill with a steep drop to one side, we slid helplessly and were only saved by the road magically turning out to have a gravel base. From then on, to the main road at Pul-i-Sefid, there was no danger, but the rain continued until we had nearly reached Tehran, and we were home by 11.30 p.m., the Embassy servants running out to greet us, and to unload the sacks, boxes and saddles we had carried.

Chapter Eighteen

A Ride to the Caspian, April 1971

The first day of the last trip that we made in Iran, started in Tehran's warm sunshine, and ended in a high mountain village in a snowstorm. We had arranged with an Iranian friend to go to his summer village above the Caspian, and we hoped that going so early in the year (April) would not be difficult and would be worth while. It was well worth while but it was difficult. We left Tehran at 8.30 a.m. with Lev and our driver in the landrover. At one o'clock we had reached the Sefid Rud dam and a little beyond, at a wayside restaurant on the outskirts of Manjil, we saw our host waiting for us with his cousin, who was accompanying us as far as the village, belonging to him, where we would spend the first night. While we lunched together in a large bare room, newly-painted in our honour, we were joined by two gendarmes who were to guard us on our journey, partly out of politeness to Denis' official position, partly because of recent trouble in the district we were to visit.

We had been told that we were to drive along a side-road to the first village, then ride for three hours the next day to another village higher up, and finally for three hours more down to the Caspian level. This was optimistic, as it turned out that there was a one-and-a-half hour ride to be done this first day, as the road petered out. Turning off the main Tehran-

Resht road to the right, it ran along the valley of the Sefid Rud, high on the east bank, with a beautiful view and still in sunshine until we suddenly ran into a thick mountain mist, which we were told had followed a day of rain on the Caspian. The village where we were to get to our mules was shrouded in this mist, and the wide paths which served as streets between the wooden houses were deep in mud, through which we struggled in gum-boots, or those without them clung to the fences or verandah posts on each side. Mr Alibuyeh and his cousin Mr Darakshan had prepared the way before us by messengers, too well, and we climbed to the shelter of an upstairs room in one of the houses to find a second lavish lunch prepared for us: however we took the opportunity of changing in this house into riding clothes and warm sweaters as it had become cold, and drank some tea, while Mr Alibuyeh, tall, grey-haired and slightly stooping, hovered over us and exclaimed in amused surprise each time a new dish arrived. The poor family, tenants of Mr Darakshan, had cooked an almost identical meal to the one we had had an hour ago, in their small kitchen; chicken kebab, liver, egg-plant, celery, and so on: we hoped that they were paid for it. After our tea we set out for a road-side coffee house just above the village, where the mules were waiting. The landrover left us there and we heard later from the driver that he took three-and-a-half hours to reach the main road, in the mist and the dark, and could not return to Tehran that night.

It was light when we set off, and a ride of an hour-and-a-half did not seem long, in spite of the mist which made visibility only about twenty yards. We were on pack saddles, as Lev had no time to put his own saddles on the mules and they had to be tied on with the baggage. Pack saddles, or *palangs*, are wide and high with no stirrups and after a time one's legs get very stiff, stretched on each side, though they are like easy chairs, with a dip in the middle in which to sit.

The mud road soon narrowed to a track, and climbed very steeply over a rocky shoulder, nine of us were riding as we had gained two more gendarmes, and our bags and Lev's

Lev, mounted on right

saddles were on two more mules, while the muleteers ran beside us. Mr Alibuyeh and Mr Javanbahkt, who had hardly changed from their Tehran suits, but just added over-coats, rode with us to begin with, Mr J. holding a paper bag with Kleenex and a 'toilet roll' he had bought down on the main road, but this went with the baggage when it was getting too damp, as the mist turned to a light rain. The gendarmes rode in front and behind, their rifles on their backs and themselves well protected by khaki capes.

Before it got dark we could see that the ground was covered with flowers; primroses, crocuses, violets and scillas. Then with the darkness it began to snow, an hour after we had started. I got separated from the party, some were behind and some in front and I could only dimly hear the bells on the mules' harness, as mine plodded on with the muleteer beside him. One could only see ahead for a few yards, and the track was covered with low bushes and stunted trees. Once we could hear a flock of sheep or goats but could not see them. The muleteer kept warm by walking but his thin clothes and shoes were soaking wet. After about half-an-hour of jogging along, cold and wet, I caught up with the soldiers ahead: at first they were just pear-like shapes with their rifles sticking up above them, peaked caps pulled down . . . in the falling snow, with Mr A slouched on his mule, Denis and Lev on theirs, and in the dusk, we looked like a drawing of the retreat from Moscow! Arriving at last at a village, all we could see was the square shapes of houses, unlit even by oil lamps, as it was late, and dogs came out barking, but not a solitary human being.

Only at the end of the 'street' it seemed, was a house with a lighted window, and dim figures rushed out to greet us, and to assist us to dismount, stiff and wet. A woman in a high, Kurdish head-dress, coloured full skirts and a man's jacket, lifted me off my mule and led me up steps to the balcony which ran round the upper floor. Soon we were all assembled, Alibuyeh, Javanbakht, Denis, Lev and I in a small cosy room, carpeted and with a bright wood fire burning. The furniture consisted of a few metal chairs and a table, and hooks on the wall served for our clothes. The windows were shuttered, without glass, but well fitted. We stood round the fire, our clothes steaming and gradually dried ourselves off, while the woman brought a big bowl, and a jug full of hot water which she poured over my feet, massaging them back to life. No-one had anticipated this weather, since Alibuyeh and Javanbakht had never been up to their villages except in summertime. Mr Javanbakht said his mother came every year, but he himself came less and less. The villagers who remained all the year round to look after the sheep and the crops were still faithful retainers of his though no longer his tenants as the land had been taken from him.

After drying as well as we could, and spreading things out which we hoped would be dry by morning, we ate a well-cooked dinner with red wine which we had contributed, and felt better. The soldiers were camped round a brazier in the next room. Going past them and out at the back of the house to the end of the balcony to the lavatory everything was white and hazy, and we carried a paraffin light in turns to avoid falling off the balcony. After dinner a bed appeared for me and a thick quilt for Denis, and on these we put our sleeping bags and blankets. On these trips it is not possible to wash more than ones hands and face. The only bath is the public one, heated once a week, usually a semi-underground, primitive structure where everyone dips in the same water.

Lev retired to sleep with the other men, and we slept well, with the fire dying slowly. In the morning it was cold and frosty and we could see only for fifty yards, but after we had set out, saying goodbye to the faithful servants and to the old lady who had come in to light the fire before breakfast, and then kissed me fondly when we left, we climbed slowly – this time with Lev's comfortable saddles – up into the snow and the sunshine at 6,000 feet. Below was a sea of cloud, about as large as the Lake of Geneva, hiding our village and all but the mountain tops. We walked on a grassy plain, again carpeted with violets and primroses, scillas and crocuses which we could now see in full light. After an hour we had to leave this plain and enter the cloud to find the village where we would have lunch (the whole distance taking three hours) and gradually we were splashing along in mud again. We met only flocks of sheep with noisy dogs, and the muleteers told us that wolves attacked frequently in winter. Mr Alibuyeh rode always in a neat blue suit, and only the pullover under the coat differed from his daily dress in Tehran. He was always courteous too, and made gentle suggestions for our comfort, asking the muleteers to adjust the saddles, and lead us where it was least slippery. Every now and then he would comment cheerfully on the landscape, "*Moi, j'aime beaucoup les petits moutons . . . ces chiens sauvages les gardent très bien . . . heureusement le temps fait un peu mieux . . .*", but on the whole we rode in silence, and only the muleteers kept up their conversation amongst us.

The lunch-time village was a sea of mud, the mules and my little grey horse sinking in up to their knees at every step, and the muleteers leaping the wooden stockades at either side to walk on less used ground. At one point I asked to walk on grass, but they rightly said that the horse could not grip as the borders were sloping, and the mud was more even. In Asiabad, we stopped at a house in the centre of the village, whose owner had also come from Tehran to greet us. I slept, as did the gendarmes, while lunch was being prepared, it was cold and we lay near braziers. After a time a man brought a beautifully handmade gun, which he had made himself, to show Lev, who had hopes of buying one to replace another, which like this one had been inlaid with mother-of-pearl.

After lunch we moved on, being assured that in two hours we should reach Mr Alibuyeh's village, and by a flat, less mountainous road. The mist cleared slowly and we were in country like the South Downs, with the same Spring flowers, and after two hours we did reach Deylamen, the biggest village so far. It had a market square which soon filled with people at the approach of their one-time landlord. We all dismounted except for Mr Alibuyeh (Mr Javanbakht had said goodbye at Damash to go back to Tehran, full of foreboding for our journey onwards, and certainly if it had continued to snow and there had been a strong wind we might have had to turn back). Mr Alibuyeh remained perched on his mule, a balaclava hat on his head rolled up above his ears, and listened to the greetings of his friends. From Deylamen a dozen of them accompanied us on foot, and Denis walked with the local doctor, a young man whom we had met the year before, now finishing his term in the government health service and leaving Deylamen for a spell in America, his first trip abroad, and a great contrast it would be.

In half-an-hour we had reached Espayli, the last village before the descent to the Caspian, where Mr Alibuyeh's family had opened their house, or a few rooms of it, for us. Espayli is on a hill above Deylamen, we had seen it in the autumn the year before, a busy 'hill station' for Caspian villagers, who used to come up to avoid the malaria at the coast in the summer, and still do, to manage their land and sheep and cattle. But now it was almost empty, only some watch dogs, a few young girls and some shepherds were moving about in the clinging mist. But once again we had a cosy room with a wood stove, and after a meal at which the doctor joined us, we slept soundly. We had whisky to warm us too, which the villagers are quite used to foreigners drinking, but seldom accept themselves.

Next morning, still in the damp mist, we set off towards the Caspian. After a few miles along the bare hill tops we started the descent, at first on open ground with scrub, then the scrub became bushes, and the bushes trees. The path zigzags steeply, we had been this way before and so could look forward to reaching a stream, watching it grow to a river as we wound down beside it, above it, crossing and re-crossing it, at times by a water-fall which drowned the shouted conversation of the muleteers. We passed more travellers on this route, and the sight of the leading animal round a far corner would mean the quick decision of the right of way if the path were narrow. The mist gave way to light rain with better visibility and in an hour or two we were in thick forest, of oak, beech, fir, box-wood, and even holly. By eleven we had reached the only tea-house on the way down, where we could stop and rest on cushions on the clean-swept boards of the balcony, and drink tea while our mules waited below, and one by one the pack mules which followed us arrived to join them. This tea house was kept by a hunter, who knew all the ways of the forest, and knew it in all seasons. His wife and daughters cooked for travellers who could spend the night if they wished or if they had to in a large, low room, carpeted and lined with the bolsters and rolled-up quilts which serve as bedding, behind the balcony. Chickens and dogs ran about in the mud on the wide track which passed the door, where mules could be loaded, unloaded, re-loaded, or stabled underneath the house. On our last visit I had brought a pair of socks from the lady of the house, made by herself, and she remembered this, especially as I was wearing them this time.

We continued down the wooded valley, and after two more hours we reached the road and Mrs Alibuyeh with the landrover to drive us to their house. She was thankful to see us having met Mr Javanbahkt in Teheran and heard of the bad weather we had set off in. She had a large lunch ready for us and a welcome bath in her bath house to which we all went in turns. The house was in the small town of Siakal, near Lahijan, and all through the afternoon we were visited by local dignitaries and relations of the Alibuyehs, including the owners of the house we had stayed in the night before in Espayli. The house was in Persian style, with the simplest of western amenities, so that we were not brought back too violently to every day life and could still think of the misty hill tracks, the neatly stepping mules, the grunts of the muleteers, the swinging skirts and thonged sandals of the peasants, the smell and stillness of the Caspian forests which we had seen for the last time in this present stay in Persia.

Epilogue

In 1973 we re-visited Roumania, after thirty-three years. Instead of taking a week to get there, and many years to return to England, we arrived with our package tour in Constanţa, four hours after leaving Gatwick airport.

The long, one-time solitary beach of Mamaia, was solid with hotels for tourists, and the dusty country lane which had led to it was a wide asphalted motor-way. Constanţa itself had grown, with factories and workers flats surrounding it on the land side. But down by the harbour we came on the Piaţa Ovidiu, our flat, unchanged. The Mercur had gone, and the Bar Alcazar; the Post Office, which had been the centre of the street fighting in the summer of the 1940 up-rising, was a Museum, as was the huge Orthodox Patriarchate – an archaeological one. The main improvement seemed to us to be the public transport, buses running at intervals of a few minutes, in all directions, making taxis unnecessary, and there were few private cars.

After a trip to the monasteries of Moldavia by air, which we had not been able to do in the war, we went with our tour to Bucharest and the mountains of Transylvania, and spent a night in the Palace Hotel in Sinaia, where we had been on our honeymoon. The hotel had been 'modernised', or 'popularised' by the addition of brightly coloured false walls to cover the nineteenth century Corinthian columns of the hall and dining-room, and the large Casino had become a Palace of Culture.

Palaces of Culture were evident everywhere, and few cinemas
or other places of amusement, so for relaxation with the local
people we had drinks of *Tsvica* in the bars, and meals in
restaurants; but instead of the variety of previous days, the
olives, grapes, oranges and fruits of all sorts from neighbouring
Mediterranean countries, there was only one dish on the menu
and no dessert. The Palace of King Carol the First and his suc-
cessors at Sinaia was an interesting museum too, with its
laboriously carved walls and furniture, its Turkish, or Moorish,
room, and the little theatre with faded gold curtains and
upholstery.

In Bucharest some Roumanian communist acquaintances
entertained us in a pre-war restaurant, and at our request the
gypsy orchestra played a song popular in war-time days,
which for them too brought back memories, they said. The
centre of Bucharest had not changed, but again the Central
Post Office had become a museum, containing, besides remains
of Roman Dacia, the crown jewels and decorations of the late
royal family.

Back in Constanţa, peopled with ghosts as we had no way
of finding anyone we had previously known there, we were
taken to the Continental Hotel, formerly the Carlton, where
in 1940 we had been forced to stay the night because shooting
in the town had blocked the way to our flat from the restaurant
we had been in when trouble broke out. From there, on our
last day this time, we set out to look for the Hotel Francez,
scene of many social occasions on its little terrace overlooking
the sea. No-one had heard of it, but after a search we came on
a wall on which, high up, the letters 'Francez' had almost
faded, and below it was the building and tiny, weed-grown
garden where the gay, hard-working Marcoviç family we had
known best, had lived, until war and revolution overtook them.

Some years later, too, we visited Trebizond, and had not
been long in the new chromium and glass hotel opposite the
old *Yeşil Yurt*, when Hussein the younger kavass appeared;
news had gone quickly round of our arrival. He was white-
haired, but still had his trim 'handle-bar' moustache. Instead

of his uniform, which I pictured so clearly, he was wearing a neat grey suit, and carried a felt hat. We talked of old friends and I mentioned Eminé. 'Ah,' he said, pointing upwards, *Eminé gitti* (she went away).

selves at the mercy of their Hindus.

Chapter 11

Safe at Last.

This time they ~~were~~ were put in the jail of Delhi and it was awfull. But they did not quite give up hope.

for a week they lived on the dirty Prison Food and then one day as they were just thinking it was no good they heard a great noise in the yard outside and all of a sudden the door burst open. "is there any one in here" they heard some one say and to their great joy it was spoken in English. "Yes" shouted Mr Stevenson (in English, although he could speak Hindustanee).